REAL ESTATE FINANCE

IN A NUTSHELL

SIXTH EDITION

By

JON W. BRUCE

Professor of Law
Vanderbilt University

THOMSON
*
™
WEST

Mat #40617120

COPYRIGHT © 1979, 1985, 1991 WEST PUBLISHING CO.

© West, a Thomson business, 1997, 2004

© 2009 Thomson/Reuters

      610 Opperman Drive

      St. Paul, MN 55123

      1–800–313–9378

Printed in the United States of America

ISBN: 978–0–314–18354–5

TEXT IS PRINTED ON 10% POST CONSUMER RECYCLED PAPER

To my wife
Barbara Edmonson Bruce

*

III

PREFACE

This book is a concise textual treatment of the law of real estate finance. It is designed primarily to help law students negotiate a law school course on the subject. Other members of the legal community may use this work as a general reference and starting point for research. A table of secondary authorities is included to acknowledge sources and assist readers who desire more information about a topic introduced in this volume.

The material in this book is organized into detailed outline form for two reasons. First, the format is utilized to give students a thorough overview of the subject and a set of pegs upon which to hang information gleaned from classroom discussion. Second, the relative rigidity of this style helped me resist the urge to write a treatise-like work complete with mountains of footnotes. Such a volume, of course, is inconsistent with the purpose of the Nutshell Series. Exhaustive discussion, therefore, has been sacrificed in favor of summarization and clarity. Readers are requested to keep this in mind while proceeding through these materials.

One final word about the book. Real estate finance is like most property law, overgrown with rules. The principles, of course, are stated here, but so are the underlying theories. This approach is intended to afford readers a better understanding of doctrine as well as an opportunity to begin critically examining it.

I wish to say thanks to the following people—my wife Barb for her patience and understanding during the preparation of all six editions of this book; John Stark and Dan Sterner of the Indianapolis bar for giving me an excellent introduction to the practice of real estate finance law; Doug Mulligan, my research assistant on the first edition, for his tireless efforts; Jim Gillespie for his encouragement and helpful comments on the first edition; Scott Sartin, my research assistant on the fourth edition, for his conscientious assistance; Jim Ely, a Vanderbilt colleague, for his valuable suggestions about the third through sixth editions; law librarians, editors, faculty-support staff, and others for their help with this and prior editions.

JON W. BRUCE

Vanderbilt Law School
November 2008

OUTLINE

OUTLINE

OUTLINE

TABLE OF CASES

References are to Pages

TABLE OF CASES

REAL ESTATE FINANCE

IN A NUTSHELL

SIXTH EDITION

*

CHAPTER 1

INTRODUCTION TO LAW OF REAL ESTATE FINANCE

This introductory chapter presents an overview of the law of real estate finance. Because the mortgage is the cornerstone of real estate finance, it is the focal point of this chapter and for that matter the entire book.

I. MORTGAGE CONCEPT

A. DEFINITION AND DESCRIPTION

A mortgage is the transfer of an interest in land as security, usually for the repayment of a loan, but occasionally for the performance of another obligation. The typical mortgage transaction is relatively uncomplicated. A landowner borrows money from an institutional lender and enters a written agreement with the lender that the landowner's real estate is collateral for the loan. In legal terminology the landowner-borrower is a mortgagor, the lender is a mortgagee, and the agreement is a mortgage. If the mortgagor fails to pay the mortgage loan, the mortgagee may enforce its security interest by using appropriate foreclosure procedures to have the mortgaged land sold to satisfy the debt. (In all of the illustrations in this book "MR" refers to the mortgagor and "ME" refers to the mortgagee).

B. OBLIGATION/SECURITY DISTINCTION

A mortgage exists solely as security for an underlying obligation, ordinarily a promissory note. *See* Ch. 4, pp. 74–76 (considering necessity for underlying obligation and form of obligation). Consequently, every mortgage lives, travels, and dies with the obligation it secures.

Illustration: MR executes a promissory note and a mortgage to ME. ME assigns the note to A, but through inadvertence fails to assign the mortgage to A. Nonetheless, the mortgage follows the note into A's hands by operation of law. *See* Ch. 7, pp. 132–137 (discussing assignment of mortgage loan).

Illustration: MR executes a promissory note and a mortgage to ME. MR pays ME in full. ME returns the note to MR, but ME does not release the mortgage. ME has no further rights under the mortgage. The security interest created by the mortgage lapses when the underlying debt is satisfied. *See* Ch. 4, pp. 94–101 (analyzing discharge of obligation and mortgage).

C. STATUTE OF FRAUDS

A mortgage, as the transfer of an interest in land, falls squarely within the scope of the Statute of

Frauds. Thus, mortgages, as well as agreements to execute mortgages, must be in writing to comply with the Statute. Equitable principles, however, may dictate that a mortgage arises by operation of law or is enforceable even though it is unwritten.

Illustration: Y asks Z for a loan to pay several bills. Z makes the loan upon Y's oral pledge that Y's farm is security for the loan. Y defaults. Z seeks to foreclose and have the farm sold. Z has no right to do so, because Y's oral pledge is unenforceable. As a general rule, simply lending money does not constitute sufficient part performance to take an unwritten security arrangement out of the Statute of Frauds. Hence, the loan is unsecured.

Illustration: C asks D for a loan to purchase a specific parcel of real estate. D makes the loan upon C's oral promise to give D a mortgage on the property to be purchased. C uses the loan proceeds to purchase the property, but refuses to execute a mortgage to D as promised. C defaults. D seeks to foreclose and have the land sold. D generally may do so because an equitable mortgage arises by operation of law in order to permit D to obtain payment out of the product of D's loan. Such a mortgage is not subject to the Statute of Frauds. D also might prevail on another ground. Hardship on D, advancement of the loan proceeds, and their use to purchase the property may be considered to constitute sufficient part performance to satisfy the Statute of Frauds, rendering C's oral promise enforceable.

II. HISTORICAL DEVELOPMENT OF MORTGAGE

Real estate finance is best understood by one who is thoroughly acquainted with the development of the mortgage concept. An abbreviated jaunt through legal history, therefore, is in order. During this excursion, note how the legal pendulum swings first in the mortgagee's favor, then in the mortgagor's direction, and so on, back and forth, throughout history.

A. DEFEASIBLE FEE AS FINANCING DEVICE

At early English common law, a mortgage was simply a deed of a defeasible fee from the mortgagor to the mortgagee. If the debt was repaid at maturity, or "law day" in common law parlance, the mortgagee's estate terminated, and the mortgagor again owned the land. If, however, the debt was not paid at maturity, the mortgagee's defeasible fee became a fee simple absolute. Because the law courts strictly enforced the time for payment, the mortgagor lost the land even if the mortgagor tendered payment just a day late.

B. EQUITY OF REDEMPTION

1. Creation and Growth

In order to mitigate the harsh results of this common law approach, the equity courts intervened. If a mortgagor could establish a sound reason for failing to perform as agreed in the mortgage, equity would permit the mortgagor to recover the land by paying the debt after the maturity date. This right of late payment eventually was extended to all mortgagors without regard to the existence of individual equities and became known as the equity of redemption. *See* Ch. 8, pp. 179–182 (discussing equity of redemption).

2. Preservation/Clogging

Equity courts have always zealously preserved the mortgagor's equity of redemption. Any clause in the mortgage or in a contemporaneous agreement that has the effect of eliminating or impairing the mortgagor's equitable right to redeem is termed clogging and is prohibited. Otherwise a mortgage could be transformed into a defeasible fee by the use of a simple waiver clause. The courts' protective approach in this regard gave rise to the maxim: "once a mortgage, always a mortgage."

Illustration: MR executes a mortgage to ME. At the same time, MR gives ME an option to purchase the mortgaged land for a nominal sum if MR defaults. The option is unenforceable as a contemporaneous clog on MR's equity of redemption. It is really a disguised waiver. *See* Ch. 6, pp. 121–123 (considering when mortgagee may properly acquire mortgaged property from mortgagor).

C. FORECLOSURE

1. Strict Foreclosure

The creation of an immutable equity of redemption placed the mortgagee in a difficult position. The defaulting mortgagor's right to redeem effectively prevented the mortgagee from selling or improving the mortgaged property. The English equity courts thus came to the aid of mortgagees by developing the concept of foreclosure of the equity of redemption. After default and at the mortgagee's request, the equity courts set a time period within which the mortgagor was required to pay the debt or lose the right to redeem. If the mortgagor failed to pay within the period specified, the mortgagee obtained a fee simple absolute. This method of terminating the mortgagor's equity of redemption became known as strict foreclosure.

2. Foreclosure by Sale

Strict foreclosure was inherently unfair to the mortgagor because the value of the mortgaged land acquired by the mortgagee frequently exceeded the debt. The legal pendulum, consequently, began to swing back in favor of mortgagors. This time our state courts played an active role. The rest of this chapter deals exclusively with the evolution of real estate finance law in this country.

Equity again readjusted the conflicting interests of the parties by requiring foreclosure of the mortgagor's equity of redemption via public sale. The proceeds of the foreclosure sale were distributed pursuant to equitable considerations. The funds were employed first to satisfy the mortgage debt. Any surplus was given to the mortgagor. *See* Ch. 10, p. 216 (discussing distribution of proceeds). If the funds were insufficient to pay off the debt, the mortgagee was permitted to recover a deficiency judgment against the mortgagor. *See* Ch. 10, pp. 216–217 (treating deficiency judgments).

In the United States, foreclosure by sale is the primary method of terminating the mortgagor's equity of redemption. Strict foreclosure is not widely available. *See* Ch. 10, pp. 222–223 (discussing strict foreclosure).

Two variations on the foreclosure by sale theme exist—foreclosure by judicial sale and foreclosure by power of sale. Foreclosure by judicial sale involves a court-supervised procedure that is often complex, protracted, and expensive. Nonetheless, because judicial supervision protects the mortgagor, foreclosure by judicial sale is available in all states and is the exclusive method of foreclosing the mortgagor's equity of redemption in a substantial number of jurisdictions. *See* Ch. 10, pp. 211–217 (analyzing foreclosure by judicial sale).

Power of sale foreclosure derives its name from the fact that in many jurisdictions the mortgage may include a provision granting the mortgagee the power to sell the mortgaged property without court supervision. Ch. 10, pp. 217–222 (discussing foreclosure by power of sale). Where this type of foreclosure is available, lenders frequently employ a special kind of mortgage known as a deed of trust. The deed of trust provides that a trustee will conduct the foreclosure sale outside the judicial system. *See* Ch. 3, pp. 54–55 (treating deed of trust).

D. STATUTORY REDEMPTION

Statutes in numerous jurisdictions give the mortgagor an opportunity to redeem the mortgaged property even after the mortgagor's equity of redemption has been foreclosed. This right, referred to as statutory redemption, exists in about one-half of the states. Generally the mortgagor is given a set period of time after the foreclosure sale, such as one year, to pay the foreclosure sale price and redeem the land. *See* Ch. 10, pp. 223–227 (analyzing statutory redemption).

III. MORTGAGE THEORIES

Although it is commonly recognized that a mortgage is a transfer of a security interest in land, controversy exists regarding the precise nature of the mortgagee's interest. During the evolution of the mortgage from a defeasible conveyance to a security device, courts did not adequately deal with the interrelated problem of possession. Today states handle this unresolved possession problem in three different ways.

A. TITLE THEORY

Some states, referred to as title theory jurisdictions, follow a diluted version of the original common law view that a mortgage conveys legal title to the mortgagee. Predicated on the concept that possession follows legal title, the mortgagee in these jurisdictions receives the right to possession of the mortgage property when the mortgage is executed.

Most title theory states lie in the eastern part of the country where early common law had the greatest impact. Use of the term title theory to describe the mortgage law of these jurisdictions, however, is somewhat misleading. Title theory states have departed from most aspects of the traditional English theory of mortgages, retaining it primarily with respect to possession. As a general rule, these jurisdictions consider the mortgagee's "title" to be in the nature of a security interest, rather than fee ownership.

B. INTERMEDIATE THEORY

A few states still recognize the mortgage as a conveyance of a form of legal title, but limit the mortgagee's right to possession in a manner consistent with the view that the mortgage creates merely a security interest. These states, called intermediate theory jurisdictions, give the mortgagor the right to possession until default and the mortgagee the right thereafter.

C. LIEN THEORY

In the majority of states, the mortgage is viewed as giving the mortgagee a lien on the mortgaged property, not legal title. Thus, in these lien theory jurisdictions, the mortgagor retains the right to possession until foreclosure.

D. PRACTICAL SIGNIFICANCE OF MORTGAGE THEORIES

It is important to emphasize that even in title and intermediate theory states, the mortgagee's rights as erstwhile legal titleholder generally have been eliminated where unnecessary to protect its security interest. The primary distinction among the title, intermediate and lien theories, therefore, is with respect to the right to possession. Even this difference often is obscured by a mortgage clause that spells-out the rights of the parties regarding possession. *See* Ch. 8, pp. 169–170 (discussing significance of mortgage theories).

IV. MODERN FINANCING FORMATS

Although the mortgage is still the foundation of real estate finance, many sophisticated financing variations exist today. The complex financing formats that have evolved over the past several decades may employ a combination of mortgages, leases, installment land contracts, outright conveyances, or other arrangements. In subsequent chapters, you will become well acquainted with fundamental mortgage law and will be introduced to a wide variety of other real estate financing devices.

CHAPTER 2

MORTGAGE MARKET

The principles of real estate finance law discussed in this book are meaningful only when considered in light of the practical aspects of mortgage lending. This chapter, therefore, deals with the structure and operation of the mortgage market.

I. PURPOSE OF FINANCING

A. GENERAL

The purpose of the mortgage loan is the initial point of inquiry. Distinctions in two categories are important: (1) Is the mortgage loan money to be used for construction or permanent financing? (2) Is the mortgage loan to be secured by residential or commercial property? The answers to these questions determine to a large extent the source of the loan and the terms of the mortgage agreement.

B. CONSTRUCTION/PERMANENT FINANCING

1. Descriptions and Distinction

A construction mortgage loan, sometimes referred to as an interim loan, is a short-term loan to an owner-developer for the construction of improvements on the real estate that secures the loan.

Illustration: MR is a real estate developer who wishes to build an apartment building on land MR already owns. ME loans MR money to construct the project, to be disbursed as construction progresses. The loan, secured by a mortgage on the land and improvements, is due in eighteen months. ME collects only interest during the eighteen months. This is a simplified construction mortgage loan.

A permanent mortgage loan, sometimes referred to as a final loan, is a long-term loan to the owner of the real estate that secures the loan.

Illustration: MR obtains a loan from ME to purchase a house and gives ME a mortgage on the house as security. The loan, extending for a thirty-year term, is payable in equal monthly installments of principal and interest. This is a typical residential permanent mortgage loan.

2. Relationship Between Construction Lenders and Permanent Lenders

Construction mortgage loans and permanent mortgage loans often work hand-in-hand; upon completion of construction, the construction lender is usually paid by funds obtained from a permanent lender. The construction lender then either assigns its mortgage to the permanent lender or releases the construction loan mortgage so that the permanent lender's mortgage has first lien priority. The parties involved, of course, have arranged all this ahead of time.

The following scenario is common. The borrower first obtains a loan commitment from the permanent lender, then secures construction financing. The arrangement between the borrower and the construction lender is set out in a construction loan agreement. Before construction funds are advanced, the lenders enter a buy-sell agreement whereby the permanent lender agrees to "take-out" the construction lender upon completion of construction.

3. Construction Lender's Special Risks

a. Nature of Risk and Minimizing It

A construction mortgage loan involves greater risk than a permanent mortgage loan. The construction lender's investment is fully secured only when the project is completed in accordance with the plans and specifications upon which the parties originally agreed. Thus, the construction lender must closely supervise construction and advance funds under the construction loan agreement as the project properly progresses. *See* Ch. 4, pp. 82–84 (discussing construction lender's dilemma). As compensation for assuming this burden, the construction lender charges a higher rate of interest than does the permanent lender.

The construction lender also attempts to minimize its risk of loss in the event the project should encounter construction difficulty. First, it takes steps to insure that its mortgage has first lien priority. *See* Ch. 4, pp. 76–85 (analyzing issues concerning future advances); Ch. 9, pp. 186–187 (treating recording statutes). Second, the construction lender may require the mortgagor to personally guaranty completion of construction. Third, often in lieu of the second alternative, it may call for the mortgagor to obtain performance and payment bonds in their joint names.

b. Performance and Payment Bonds

In order to be protected by performance and payment bonds, the construction lender must be named as an obligee together with the mortgagor. When this is done the bond is called a dual obligee bond.

The dual obligee performance bond assures the construction lender that the project will be completed in accordance with the construction contract. However, the coverage afforded a construction lender by a dual obligee bond is commonly limited by a savings clause, often called a Los Angeles clause, that releases the bonding company from liability if the mortgagor breaches the construction contract. Consequently, the savings clause may operate at a critical time to eliminate the construction lender's protection under the dual obligee performance bond.

The dual obligee payment bond assures the construction lender that all charges for labor or material used in construction will be paid. This prevents loss resulting from the attachment of any mechanics' liens that might gain priority over the construction loan mortgage, but at the same time raises the possibility that the bonding company may seek to be subrogated to the rights of mechanics' lienors. *See* Ch. 9, pp. 197–201 (analyzing mechanics' lien statutes). Moreover, the bond may contain a savings/Los Angeles clause. Hence, as a practical matter, the dual obligee payment bond may afford the lender no protection at all.

c. Liability for Construction Defects

In the last several decades, construction lenders have faced an unexpected additional risk—liability for faulty construction. In Connor v. Great Western Savings and Loan Association, 73 Cal.Rptr. 369 (Cal.1968), the Supreme Court of California held a construction lender liable for construction defects on a negligence theory because the lender went beyond the domain of the usual lender and actively participated in the enterprise. However, almost immediately after the *Connor* decision, the California legislature enacted a statute purporting to limit construction lenders' liability for construction defects. Cal.Civ.Code § 3434 (West 1997). Although the doctrine fashioned by the California court in *Connor* has been recognized elsewhere, it has rarely if ever been employed outside California to impose liability on a particular construction lender.

C. RESIDENTIAL/COMMERCIAL PROPERTY

The distinction between residential and commercial mortgage loans is important because some lenders specialize in making loans secured by a particular kind of property. Residential mortgage loans are loans secured by any form of residential property—for example: single-family dwellings, duplexes, apartments, or condominiums. Sometimes residential mortgage loans are further broken down into loans on one-to-four-family properties called home loans and loans on larger multi-family projects. Commercial mortgage loans are loans made on non-residential property—for example: shopping centers, hotels, office buildings, warehouses, or manufacturing plants.

II.
ORIGINATING/SERVICING/HOLDING

In order to fully understand the mortgage market, one must appreciate the differences among originating, servicing, and holding mortgage loans. The institution that initially advances funds "originates" the mortgage loan. The organization that collects the mortgage payment from and otherwise deals directly with the borrower "services" the loan. The lender that owns the mortgage loan at any one time "holds" the loan. Sometimes the same entity originates, holds, and services the loan. On many other occasions, the originator sells the mortgage loan to a new holder who hires someone, frequently the originator, to service the loan.

The right to service a mortgage loan is a valuable asset because of the fee involved and the possibility of earning interest on escrowed funds. Accordingly, a vigorous market for mortgage servicing rights exists. Indeed, several different entities may service a particular mortgage loan over its lifetime, perhaps to the consternation of the mortgagor. *See* p. 46 (discussing RESPA regulation of transfer of servicing).

III. SOURCES OF REAL ESTATE FINANCING

The institutions that make mortgage loan funds available form the core infrastructure of the mortgage market. The most significant sources of real estate financing are described in general terms in this section.

The following treatment of real estate financing sources includes discussion of periods when particular mortgage lenders were experiencing financial difficulty and what then transpired. Another such period begin in 2007 and continued in 2008. An extremely roiled mortgage environment, particularly its subprime sector, marked by a spate of foreclosures has rendered uncertain the financial well-being of some mortgage lenders. Resolution of this situation may likely to be elusive and distant notwithstanding legislative and administrative efforts by the federal government in 2008 to rectify the housing/mortgage market. *See* pp. 35–37 (analyzing mortgage insurance and guaranty programs); pp. 37–39 (treating secondary mortgage market support institutions); pp. 48–49 (discussing Housing and Economic Recovery Act of 2008); pp. 49–50 (consid-

ering Emergency Economic Stabilization Act of
2008).

A. COMMERCIAL BANKS

Commercial banks are depository institutions
chartered by either a state or the federal government. Although commercial banks make a substantial number of permanent mortgage loans,
traditionally they have limited such long-term investments in order to maintain liquidity to meet
demand deposits. Construction lending is usually a
more significant part of their mortgage loan operation; the yields are higher, and the bank's funds
are not tied up for prolonged periods.

By 1990, numerous commercial banks were in
financial difficulty. Many of their mortgage loans
were in jeopardy because of overbuilding and a
sluggish real estate market. Bankers and regulators
took various steps to avert further trouble. By the
mid–1990s, the mortgage lending situation for commercial banks had improved.

B. SAVINGS AND LOAN ASSOCIATIONS

Savings and loan associations, or savings associations, are also either state or federally chartered.
They are specialists in housing finance and heavily
invest in both construction and permanent residential mortgages.

In the late 1980s, the savings and loan system
entered a state of crisis. Many institutions became

insolvent, and numerous others teetered on the brink of collapse. As part of the Financial Institutions Reform, Recovery and Enforcement Act of 1989, Congress created the Resolution Trust Corporation (RTC) to depose of the assets of failed savings and loan associations. These assets included construction loan mortgages, permanent mortgages, and a significant amount of real estate obtained from defaulting mortgagors. The RTC completed its work in late 1995 and discontinued business the last day of that year.

C.　MUTUAL SAVINGS BANKS

Mutual savings banks, or savings banks, are state or federally chartered institutions located primarily in the northeast. They operate in the same general sphere as savings and loan associations, but tend to concentrate their mortgage investments in permanent residential mortgages acquired from other institutional lenders.

D.　LIFE INSURANCE COMPANIES

Life insurance companies are state chartered and subject to local insurance law. Because of a relatively predictable flow of funds, life insurance companies are heavily involved in permanent financing of both commercial and multi-unit residential projects.

The long-term nature of their mortgage investments, however, puts life insurance companies in a difficult position during periods of rapid inflation.

As a consequence, they may require the right to participate in income from the project being financed. *See* Ch. 4, pp. 90–91 (discussing revenue/equity participation).

E.   PENSION FUNDS

Public and private employee pension funds are an increasing source of capital for real estate financing, particularly in the area of permanent commercial mortgages and mortgage-backed securities.

F.   REAL ESTATE INVESTMENT TRUSTS

Real estate investment trusts (REITs) are a product of federal tax legislation of the early 1960s designed to give the small investor an opportunity to participate in sophisticated and diverse real estate investments. If a REIT meets a number of tax requirements, it will not be taxed on income and capital gains distributed to its shareholders.

The first qualified REITs were "equity" trusts that developed or purchased income producing commercial property. They were not generally successful. In the late 1960s, however, REITs that engaged solely in mortgage lending became popular. Although mortgage REITs made permanent loans, they achieved importance primarily as suppliers of construction financing. Consequently, the building slump of the middle 1970s hit mortgage REITs hard. Some went bankrupt, and many others barely survived.

REITs made a comeback in the 1980s and 1990s. Equity REITs led the resurgence, and by the mid–1990s, mortgage REITs had regained a solid position in the world of mortgage lending.

G. MORTGAGE BANKING COMPANIES

Mortgage banking companies are incorporated and operated under state law. Although mortgage bankers are a source of some real estate financing funds, they are more important as intermediaries between borrowers and other lenders.

Mortgage bankers perform their intermediary function in two major ways. First, they originate home mortgage loans for sale to institutional investors and then service the loan for the investor who holds it. Second, they put commercial borrowers, construction lenders, and permanent lenders in contact with one another.

In performing the latter role, mortgage bankers often facilitate the overall operation of a transaction by financing the project for a short time between the completion of construction and the sale of the loan to the permanent investor. They frequently obtain funds for such interim financing from a commercial bank under a line of credit secured by an assignment of the mortgage loans involved. This arrangement is known as mortgage warehousing. *See* Ch. 7, pp. 160–161 (analyzing assignment of mortgage loan as security). Mortgage bankers also utilize this financing technique to enable them to serve as construction lenders in their own right. In either case the mortgage banker realizes a profit from mortgage warehousing by borrowing money, often at the commercial bank's prime interest rate, and then lending it to the developer at a higher rate of return.

H.   OTHER SOURCES

Credit unions, individuals, syndications, service corporations, state development agencies, and community housing authorities are other less significant sources of real estate investment capital.

1.   Credit Unions

State and federal credit unions offer residential mortgage loans. Moreover, certain federal credit unions have made substantial mortgaged-based investments.

2.   Sellers

Individual sellers sometimes take back a purchase money mortgage on the property being sold. These transactions, however, constitute only a small percentage of the total mortgage loans outstanding at any one time.

3.   Syndications

Syndications are groups of individual real estate investors often formed as limited partnerships. They, however, commonly invest by purchasing realty rather than by making mortgage loans.

4.   State Development Agencies

State development agencies have been created by many state legislatures to deal with intrastate housing problems by financing the construction of low-and-moderate-income housing. These development agencies generally have the power to raise funds by issuing tax-exempt bonds.

5.   Community Housing Authorities

Many cities have established a housing authority that finances the construction of low-and-moderate-income housing from the sale of tax-exempt bonds.

I.   MORTGAGE BROKERS

Mortgage brokers deserve consideration in this section even though they typically do not serve as a source of funds for real estate financing. Instead, the primary business of mortgage brokers is to arrange loan transactions between borrowers and mortgage lenders. Mortgage brokers thus contribute to mortgage market efficiency, particularly in the residential area, by performing a significant coordination/administrative function. Mortgage brokers have been involved in an increasing number of mortgages over the years and frequently receive a controversial type of remuneration—a portion of loan interest called the yield spread premium.

IV. OBTAINING REAL ESTATE FINANCING

A. APPLICATION AND COMMITMENT

Once a potential source of funds is identified, the borrower secures the mortgage loan through the process of application and commitment. The borrower initiates the process by making a formal or informal mortgage loan application to the lender who evaluates it in light of the risk involved.

The risk in mortgage financing is a two-tier one. The lender initially must assess the borrower's financial position with a view to predicting the likelihood that the underlying obligation will be repaid. Next, the lender must anticipate default and decide whether the mortgaged property will produce a sufficient amount at a foreclosure sale to pay the mortgage debt.

If the lender determines that the overall risk is acceptable, it will issue a mortgage loan commitment detailing the amount, duration, interest rate, and other pertinent items. Loans to financially weaker borrowers on less favorable terms are categorized as subprime. The length, formality, and specificity of the commitment vary from lender to lender and loan to loan. Commercial loan commitments naturally are rather complex and commonly include a provision for a nonrefundable commitment fee.

A loan commitment contains numerous terms and conditions not found in the application. Consequently, the typical commitment constitutes a counteroffer to make a loan. When the borrower accepts the commitment, a binding contract for a mortgage loan is created.

B.   MORTGAGE LOAN CONTRACT

Mortgage loan contracts have been a source of litigation. Two areas are particularly controversial: nonrefundable commitment fees and the borrower's remedy for breach.

1.   Nonrefundable Commitment Fees

The commitment fee issue arises when a borrower decides not to go through with the loan and then demands return of the "nonrefundable" commitment fee on the ground the lender has done nothing to earn it. Courts have consistently rejected this contention and held that the lender is entitled to the commitment fee either as liquidated damages for breach of contract or as compensation for keeping money available for loan to the borrower.

2.   Borrower's Remedy for Lender's Breach

On the other hand, when the lender refuses to complete the loan in accordance with the commitment, questions arise regarding the borrower's remedy for breach of contract. Although the transfer of a security interest in real property is an aspect of the contemplated loan, the borrower ordinarily is not entitled to specific performance. Damages at law are normally considered adequate to compensate the borrower for any loss the borrower may have suffered by reason of the lender's failure to advance the promised funds. Nevertheless, the borrower should be entitled to specific performance of the mortgage loan contract when the borrower is unable to obtain a similar loan elsewhere.

V. LOAN PARTICIPATION AND MORTGAGE–BACKED SECURITIES

A. LOAN PARTICIPATION

A lender is sometimes presented with the opportunity to make an attractive loan, but does not have the entire loan amount conveniently available. Instead of losing the loan, the lender may ask other lenders to provide a share of the funds. An arrangement of this kind is known as a loan participation. The originating mortgagee is the "lead" lender; the others are participants. The participants' interests in the loan are usually evidenced by participation certificates issued by the lead lender who holds the loan documents, collects payments, and disburses the appropriate share of the payments to each investor. *See* Ch. 7, p. 150 (discussing forms of loan participation).

B. MORTGAGE–BACKED SECURITIES

A special type of participation involves the sale of undivided interests in a large pool of mortgage loans. The Government National Mortgage Association (GNMA or popularly Ginnie Mae), Fannie Mae (previously the Federal National Mortgage Association or FNMA), and Freddie Mac (previously the Federal Home Loan Mortgage Corporation or FHLMC) utilize such mortgage-backed securities to stimulate private investment in housing. *See* pp. 37–39 (treating these institutions).

GNMA's "pass-through" program is an early and well-known example of this type of participation. In that program, a mortgage lender issues securities backed by a pool of mortgages. The pool is comprised of mortgages insured by FHA or guaranteed by VA. *See* pp. 35–37 (analyzing mortgage insurance and guaranty programs). The periodic mortgage payments made by mortgagors in the pool are distributed among the investors (participants) in proportion to their investments. GNMA guarantees that the investors will be paid even if mortgagors in the pool fail to make their mortgage payments.

Mortgage securitization has blossomed over time. Fannie Mae and Freddie Mac became active in the field by issuing mortgage-backed securities and guaranteeing these securities themselves. Private issuers also entered the marketplace with a range of offerings. Various forms of mortgage-backed securities have evolved, commonly involving conventional mortgages. In sum, mortgage-backed securities have achieved a substantial and increasingly important position in the mortgage market.

VI.   SECONDARY FINANCING

Several lenders may independently acquire separate security interests in the same property by utilizing the mortgage market technique known as secondary financing.

A. THE BASICS

1. Creation of Junior Mortgages

Because the modern mortgage is just a security interest in land, a landowner is free to mortgage the same property to as many lenders as are willing to make mortgage loans to the landowner. The placing of a second, third, or even fourth mortgage on land is termed secondary financing. The second and subsequent mortgages are categorized as junior mortgages. *See* Ch. 6, pp. 130–131 (considering further encumbrance of mortgaged property); Ch. 9, pp. 186–187 (analyzing general principles of priority and recording statutes); Ch. 10, p. 216 (discussing distribution of foreclosure sale proceeds).

Illustration: MR executes a mortgage to ME–1. MR then executes a second mortgage to ME–2 and finally a third mortgage to ME–3. All mortgages are valid. MR gave ME–1 only a security interest in the land, not ownership. The second and third mortgages held by ME–2 and ME–3 are referred to as junior mortgages.

Illustration: O owns a house subject to a $40,000 mortgage held by B bank. O desires to sell the house for $70,000. P agrees to purchase it at that price, but has no ready cash and is unable to obtain a first mortgage loan for the full amount of the purchase price. The parties, therefore, agree to the following arrangement in order to insure that the sale is consummated. O conveys the house to P subject to the existing $40,000 mortgage that P assumes and agrees to pay. *See* Ch. 6, pp. 111–130 (treating conveyance of mortgaged property and due-on-sale clause). P gives O a $30,000 promissory note for the balance of the purchase price and a second mortgage on the house as security for payment of that note. B bank's $40,000 first mortgage and O's $30,000 second mortgage are both valid liens on the property.

2. Importance of Mortgagor's "Equity"

Lenders should make junior mortgage loans only if the market value of the mortgaged property exceeds the unpaid balance of prior mortgages. The difference is known as the mortgagor's equity. The use of the term "equity" in this context is really a convenient way of stating the value of the mortgagor's equity of redemption.

A mortgagor's equity may accumulate in two ways: (1) the principal balance due on existing mortgage loans may be reduced by partial payment; (2) the mortgaged property may appreciate in value.

Illustration: MR owns a house worth $100,000. MR obtains a $100,000 loan from ME–1 secured by a mortgage on the house. (A mortgagor may be unable to obtain 100% financing, but it is assumed to be available here for purposes of illustration.) MR has $0 equity in the house, but still has an equity of redemption. Five years later the house has appreciated to a market value of $110,000, and MR has paid the principal on the mortgage note down to $90,000. MR, therefore, has $20,000 equity in the house. Needing cash,

MR obtains a $15,000 loan from ME–2 secured by a second mortgage on the house. After this transaction MR has $5,000 equity.

The preceding illustration demonstrates the general circumstances upon which the home equity loan market has developed. A home equity loan may consist of just one advance of a certain amount, as in the illustration, or involve a line of credit contemplating a series of advances over time. *See* Ch. 4, pp. 76–85 (discussing future advances). Tax considerations, i.e., the deductibility of interest paid, have fueled the popularity of home equity loans. *See* Ch. 3, pp. 53–54 (noting significance of tax considerations).

3. Risk and Rate

Junior mortgage loans involve a relatively high risk because the secondary lender's security interest extends only to the value of the land in excess of prior liens. *See* Ch. 9, pp. 186–187 (discussing general principles of priority and recording statutes). Hence, lenders generally make junior mortgage loans for a shorter term and at a higher interest rate than first mortgage loans.

Illustration: Assume the same facts as in the immediately preceding illustration except that MR fails to pay the loans to ME–1 and ME–2. Both mortgagees foreclose, and sale of the house produces $100,000 after expenses. ME–1 receives $90,000, the unpaid balance on the first mortgage loan. ME–2 receives $10,000. In reality, ME–2's $15,000 second mortgage loan was only partially secured. *See* Ch. 10, pp. 216–217 (treating distribution of foreclosure sale proceeds and deficiency judgment).

B.   BEYOND THE BASICS/WRAPAROUND MORTGAGES

The wraparound mortgage is an innovation in secondary financing. This financing device can be used either to derive additional funds from mortgaged real estate or to finance the purchase of such property. In either case, the wraparound mortgage is like a typical second mortgage in that it attaches to realty already encumbered by a mortgage. *See* Ch. 6, pp. 130–131 (considering further encumbrance of mortgaged property). Its unique feature is that the face amount of the wraparound mortgage is equal to the amount actually disbursed to the mortgagor plus the unpaid balance of the prior encumbrance. The mortgagor's payments on the wraparound mortgage, therefore, cover both the money advanced under the wraparound mortgage and the amount due on the first mortgage. The wraparound mortgagee takes a portion of the payment it receives and makes the necessary payment on the original mortgage.

The interest rate on the face amount of the wraparound mortgage is generally higher than the rate on the existing mortgage. The result is that the wraparound mortgagee receives a higher than stated interest rate on the money actually advanced. This is because it collects an interest differential on the first mortgage payments as they pass through its hands, in addition to interest on the funds it disbursed. At the same time, the wraparound mortgagor pays less interest than would have accrued on alternative forms of financing.

Illustration: Several years ago MR mortgaged an office building to ME–1 as security for a $1,000,000 loan at 9% interest per annum. MR has paid the mortgage loan down to $700,000 and now desires to get the $300,000 "equity" out of the project. (In this illustration it is assumed that the office building has had a constant value of $1,000,000 and that 100% financing is available.) MR could refinance by borrowing $1,000,000 at the current interest rate of 12%, paying off the first mortgage and using the $300,000 as MR desires. As an alternative, MR could obtain a conventional second mortgage loan of $300,000 at the current interest rate of 15%. MR, however, would like to avoid the significant increase in interest rate that would occur by use of either alternative. MR, therefore, obtains a wraparound mortgage loan from W–ME in the amount of $1,000,000 at 11% interest. W–ME disburses only $300,000 to MR, but receives payments from MR covering both the $300,000 advanced and the unpaid balance of the first mortgage, all at 11% interest. W–ME passes the payments on the first mortgage to ME–1 after removing the interest differential (2%). W–ME thereby receives 11% interest on the $300,000 advanced and 2% on the $700,000 balance on the first loan, an overall interest rate well in excess of the stated rate of 11%. At the same time MR pays only 11% on the $1,000,000, 1% below the current interest rate on first mortgage loans.

Illustration: O owns a farm subject to a first mortgage in favor of ME–1. MR purchases the farm from O. MR assumes the first mortgage and executes a wraparound mortgage to O in the amount of the purchase price less the down payment. This transaction is a purchase money wraparound mortgage. It is structured and administered the same as the wraparound mortgage described in the immediately preceding illustration.

VII.   FEDERAL GOVERNMENT INVOLVEMENT IN FINANCING PROCESS

Since the Depression, Congress frequently has addressed housing concerns and other matters related to real estate finance. Its activity in these areas has had a considerable impact on the mortgage market. This section discusses the federal government's involvement in the real estate financing process via housing subsidies, mortgage insurance, secondary mortgage market support institutions, and various legislative measures.

A.   HOUSING SUBSIDIES

Some Congressional action in the real estate finance area is designed to produce more and better housing for low-and-moderate-income families through housing subsidies administered by the Department of Housing and Urban Development. The form of the subsidy varies greatly from program to program.

B.   MORTGAGE INSURANCE AND GUARANTY PROGRAMS

A less direct but highly significant form of government involvement in the real estate financing process is found in the federal mortgage insurance and guaranty programs administered by the Federal Housing Administration (FHA) and the Department of Veterans Affairs (VA). These programs encourage private institutional lenders to make residential mortgage loans to borrowers who otherwise might not qualify. This is accomplished by insuring or guarantying mortgagees against loss on certain residential loans. In essence, the insurance or guaranty takes the place of a large down-payment.

Mortgage loans that are insured or guaranteed by FHA or VA are termed "FHA mortgages" or "VA mortgages" respectively. All other mortgage loans are referred to as "conventional mortgages" whether or not they are covered by private mortgage insurance.

Although FHA and VA mortgages are similar, they differ in the following generally described ways. First, FHA mortgage loans may be obtained by members of the general public. VA mortgage loans are available only to veterans. Second, FHA primarily insures eligible mortgage loans. VA issues a guaranty of partial repayment. VA borrowers, therefore, do not pay mortgage insurance premiums, as do FHA borrowers. However, VA borrowers must pay a funding fee.

A substantial segment of the FHA Modernization Act of 2008, known as the Building American Homeownership Act of 2008 (Pub. L. No. 110–289, §§ 2111–2133), is devoted to revising the traditional FHA program of mortgage insurance. Furthermore, the HOPE for Homeowners Act of 2008 (Pub. L. No. 110–289, §§ 1401–1404) establishes an FHA insurance scheme for "refinanced eligible mortgage(s)" to assist certain mortgagors with refinancing. *See* pp. 48–49 (discussing Housing and Economic Recovery Act of 2008).

Private companies also have entered the field of mortgage insurance. They gained widespread acceptance in the mortgage insurance marketplace partly by processing applications in a more efficient manner than either FHA or VA. The growth of private mortgage insurance made high loan-to-value, e.g., ninety or ninety-five percent, conventional home mortgage loans broadly available. Today private mortgage insurance companies dominate the residential mortgage insurance business.

The Homeowners Protection Act of 1998 (12 U.S.C.A. § 4901 *et seq.*) allows mortgagors to cancel private mortgage insurance on post-July 28, 1999 home mortgages if certain conditions are meet. Moreover, the Act generally requires termination of private mortgage insurance on such mortgages whenever the mortgage debt declines to seventy-eight percent of the mortgaged property's date-of-mortgage-execution value. Private mortgage insurance that survives the operation of these provisions is terminated whenever a covered mortgage's amortization schedule hits the halfway mark, provided that the mortgagor is not in default. The Act also imposes extensive disclosure requirements on mortgagees. This legislative measure is designed to relieve homeowners of the obligation to continue to submit premiums for insurance no longer needed by mortgagees.

C.　SECONDARY MORTGAGE MARKET SUPPORT INSTITUTIONS

Congress also has created several institutions designed to maintain a national secondary market for residential mortgages. The policy underlying this secondary mortgage market approach is that the support institutions can promote the even distribution of real estate investment capital throughout the country by buying mortgages from originators and selling them to investors. Distinguish the secondary mortgage market which involves the sale of first mortgages from the separate concept of secondary financing, addressed earlier this chapter, which involves the creation of junior mortgages on already encumbered land. *See* pp. 28–34 (discussing secondary financing).

The institutions charged with responsibility for maintaining a viable secondary mortgage market are Fannie Mae (previously the Federal National Mortgage Association or FNMA), the Government National Mortgage Association (GNMA or popularly Ginnie Mae), and Freddie Mac (previously the Federal Home Loan Mortgage Corporation or FHLMC.) Each organization plays a major role in this loosely constructed system.

Created near the end of the Depression, Fannie Mae is the oldest element of the secondary mortgage market. Originally part of FHA, it became privately owned, but subject to considerable governmental regulation and control. Fannie Mae buys and sells FHA, VA, and conventional mortgages in order to improve the nationwide distribution of investment capital available for mortgage financing. Fannie Mae is active in issuing mortgage-backed securities.

GNMA, a 1968 spin-off from Fannie Mae, is a government owned entity within the Department of Housing and Urban Development. GNMA has engaged in a variety of market support activities. It notably is involved in the secondary mortgage market via special mortgage investment programs such as the "pass-through" mortgage-backed securities program discussed earlier in this chapter. *See* pp. 27–28 (discussing mortgage-backed securities).

Freddie Mac has operated as a privately owned corporation heavily regulated by the federal government. It was created in 1970 to establish a viable secondary mortgage market for conventional mortgages. Freddie Mac performs this function in good part by assembling pools of conventional mortgages and selling securities backed by these pooled mortgages. It also may acquire FHA and VA mortgages.

The roiled mortgage environment of 2007–2008 eroded the financial underpinnings of Fannie Mae and Freddie Mac. See pp. 18–19 (introducing sources of real estate financing). In 2008, the federal government took steps to ensure the viability of these key institutions. Indeed, a substantial portion of the Federal Housing Finance Regulatory Reform Act of 2008 (Pub. L. No. 110–289, §§ 1001–1605) is designed to fortify Fannie Mae and Freddie Mac through various means such as enhanced regulation, increased credit, and authorization for the federal government to purchase their stock. *See* pp. 48–49 (discussing Housing and Economic Recovery Act of 2008). Moreover, shortly after this measure was enacted, Fannie Mae and Freddie Mac went into a federal-agency-administered conservatorship. This arrangement is part of a revitalization scheme for Fannie Mae and Freddie Mac predicated on extensive federal government involvement including loans, preferred stock acquisition, mortgage-backed securities purchases, and common stock acquisition rights.

D.   OTHER GOVERNMENT INVOLVEMENT

Over the years Congress has enacted laws on a variety of other real estate finance subjects. The following legislative measures have had an impact on the mortgage market.

1. Truth in Lending

The Truth in Lending Act of 1968 (15 U.S.C.A. § 1601 *et seq.*), implemented by the Board of Governors of the Federal Reserve System via Regulation Z, requires lenders to disclose financing costs and terms to prospective borrowers. As a general rule, Truth in Lending applies only to consumer credit transactions involving $25,000 or less. Business or commercial loans for any amount are not covered.

Many real estate credit transactions are governed by Truth in Lending. Although business or commercial real estate loans are, of course, exempt, the Act applies to consumer real estate loans regardless of amount. The $25,000 ceiling was removed from this type of transaction so that the average home-buyer is protected when embarking upon the only large-scale financing arrangement that person may ever enter.

As a general matter, the creditor in a standard real estate credit transaction must make the usual disclosure for closed-end transactions including a statement of the amount financed, the finance charge, and the annual percentage rate. Significant differences exist, however, between its disclosure obligations and those of a creditor in a non-real estate transaction. For example, the items to be included in computing the finance charge differ. Moreover, the real estate creditor must state whether the mortgage loan may be assumed. Further, in certain real estate credit transactions the borrower has a right to rescind that must be disclosed. If the transaction creates a lien on the debtor's principal dwelling that secures a non-acquisition or non-construction loan, the consumer may rescind the transaction within three business days after closing or after the rescission right and other material matters are disclosed, whichever is later.

Specialized disclosure requirements have been tailored for certain types of mortgage loans. Such is the case with respect to adjustable rate mortgages, reverse mortgages, closed-end home equity loans that bear a high interest/fee rate, and open-end home equity loans. *See* pp. 30–31 (discussing home equity loan); Ch. 4, pp. 87–88 (analyzing adjustable rate mortgage); Ch 4, p. 95 (considering reverse mortgage).

The Truth in Lending Act was amended by the Mortgage Disclosure Improvement Act of 2008 (Pub. L. No. 110–289, §§ 2501–2503). Among other things, this measure strengthens the disclosure scheme for adjustable rate mortgages. *See* pp. 48–49 (discussing Housing and Economic Recovery Act of 2008).

In addition to disclosure standards, Truth in Lending establishes substantive limitations on closed-end home equity loans that bear a high interest/fee rate. For example, prepayment penalties are curtailed for loans in this category. *See also* pp. 50–51 (considering predatory lending). "Higher-priced mortgage loans," which constitute a recently created separate classification, are subject to prepayment penalty constraints as well. *See* Ch. 4, pp. 99–100 (treating prepayment).

Certain dubious, rapacious, or misleading mortgage lending activities are prohibited under Truth in Lending. Closed-end home equity loans that bear a high interest/fee rate and "higher-priced mortgage loans" are the primary targets of the bulk of these protective mandates.

2. Interstate Land Sales Full Disclosure Act of 1968

Congress enacted the Interstate Land Sales Full Disclosure Act of 1968 (15 U.S.C.A. § 1701 *et seq.*) to eliminate the use of fraudulent or misleading practices in the marketing of certain types of raw land. The Act applies to developers who sell or lease unimproved subdivision lots as part of a common promotional plan in interstate commerce or through the mail. Numerous exemptions, both full and partial, are available. For example, developers of subdivisions that include less than twenty-five lots are totally exempt from the Act. Developers of subdivisions containing less than one hundred lots are exempt from the Act's registration and disclosure provisions described below, but are still subject to the Act's antifraud provisions.

Nonexempt subdivision developers must disclose the material facts about the land being offered for sale. Disclosure is accomplished by filing a statement of record with the Office of Interstate Land Sales Registration in the Department of Housing and Urban Development and by delivering a property report to prospective purchasers. The statement of record must include certain specific information about the subdivision, the surrounding area, and the developer. The property report is a condensed more readable version of the statement of record.

The Act gives the purchaser certain remedies for the developer's failure to make proper disclosure. Rescission is available in two general instances. First, if the developer fails to give the purchaser a property report prior to the execution of a sales contract, the purchaser may rescind the contract within two years of its execution. Second, even if the purchaser is furnished a property report before signing a sales contract, the purchaser may rescind the contract within seven days of its execution. (Frequently, the contract is an installment land contract. *See* Ch. 3, pp. 60–67 (analyzing installment land contracts). If so, additional disclosure and rescission provisions of the Act apply.)

The purchaser also has the right to obtain specific performance, damages, or other appropriate relief from the developer for violations of the Act. Although the Act does not apply to lending institutions engaging in the normal course of their real estate financing activities, a lender may be liable for damages if it actively participates in a plan to sell or lease property covered by the Act.

3. National Flood Insurance Program

Over the years, large amounts of federal disaster relief funds have been paid to flood victims. A substantial portion of this money has been used to rebuild structures in the same high-risk location. This situation, coupled with the general unavailability of private flood insurance, led Congress to establish the National Flood Insurance Program in 1968 (42 U.S.C.A. § 4001 *et seq.*). The Program made flood insurance available to property owners in communities that established approved land use ordinances limiting construction in flood-hazard areas.

Few communities responded voluntarily. Thus, the Flood Disaster Protection Act of 1973 was enacted. It made participation in the Program virtually mandatory by prohibiting federally regulated lending institutions from making loans secured by mortgages on structures in flood-prone areas unless the borrower obtained flood insurance. Because such insurance is available only in communities participating in the Program, cities and towns began to enact the required land use regulation. Soon flood insurance became available to property owners in most communities with areas prone to flooding.

In the late 1970s, the Program was amended to eliminate the prohibition against making mortgage loans on flood-plain property in a nonparticipating community. But by that time, the Program had taken hold throughout the country. Moreover, federally regulated lending institutions still must require mortgagors to obtain flood insurance, when available, on mortgaged structures in flood-prone areas.

The Program, which is administered by the Federal Emergency Management Agency, has been re-

vamped in various ways by Congress over the last
two decades in an ongoing effort to rectify structur-
al and implemental programmatic deficiencies. In
2007–2008, Congress again was considering over-
hauling the Program. At this writing, each house
had passed its own version of a "Flood Insurance
Reform and Modernization Act."

4. Real Estate Settlement Procedures Act of 1974

The Real Estate Settlement Procedures Act of
1974 (12 U.S.C.A. § 2601 *et seq.*), known as RESPA,
is basically a disclosure statute designed to protect
homebuyers or homeowners from the imposition of
unanticipated, unwarranted, or excessive loan closing costs. RESPA covers all "federally related mortgage loans." Most residential mortgage loans fall
within this category. As a general rule, RESPA
applies when an institutional lender makes a loan
that is secured by a mortgage, first or junior, on
one-to-four-family residential real estate.

When a lending institution receives an application
for a federally related mortgage loan it must provide the prospective borrower with: (1) a copy of a
booklet published by the Department of Housing
and Urban Development (HUD) that discusses closing costs and (2) a good faith estimate of all loan
closing costs. Then, at or before the closing, the
lender or whoever else conducts the closing must
provide both the borrower and the seller with a
completed HUD Settlement Statement setting forth
the precise amount of all closing costs. The lender
may not impose any fee or charge for the prepara-

tion or submission of any of the documents required
by the Act.

RESPA also requires that lenders disclose to ap-
plicants for federally related mortgage loans whether the servicing of the loan may be transferred.
Further, the borrower must be notified of any
transfer of servicing. *See* pp. 17–18 (analyzing differences among originating/servicing/holding and
discussing transfer of servicing rights).

In addition to these disclosure requirements,
RESPA includes significant substantive provisions.
One portion of the Act is designed to eliminate
kickbacks and unearned fees. Another section limits
the amount that a lender may require a borrower to
place in an escrow account for the payment of
casualty insurance premiums and property taxes.
See Ch. 4, pp. 96–98 (discussing escrow accounts).

5.   Home Mortgage Disclosure Act of 1975

As noted earlier in this chapter, one aspect of the
mortgage lender's risk is whether the land offered
as security is of sufficient market value to satisfy
the debt in the event the borrower defaults. *See* pp.
25–26 (discussing application and commitment process). Some lending institutions may consider all
property located in a designated area of the community they serve as inadequate or high-risk collateral
and hence, unacceptable as security for a standard
mortgage loan. This form of lending discrimination
is known as "redlining" because of the manner in
which the designated areas may have been identified on a map of the community. Typically, redlined

areas are older, integrated, middle-class or lower middle-class neighborhoods.

The Home Mortgage Disclosure Act of 1975 (12 U.S.C.A. § 2801 *et seq.*) is designed to identify and help eliminate redlining. The Act requires many financial institutions to disclose detailed information about their residential mortgage loans by reference to census tract. Such lenders also must report data regarding their loan applications. Although the Act makes redlining more visible, it does not provide a penalty for such activity. Congress apparently decided to rely on community pressure to force lenders to act responsibly in this regard. However, the Community Reinvestment Act of 1977 (12 U.S.C.A. § 2901 *et seq.*) does place an obligation on regulatory agencies to determine whether a financial institution adequately serves its community and to take this factor into consideration when examining the institution or reviewing its application for a merger, a new branch, or other special action.

6. Comprehensive Environmental Response, Compensation, and Liability Act of 1980

Congress enacted the Comprehensive Environmental Response, Compensation, and Liability Act of 1980 (42 U.S.C.A. § 9601 *et seq.*) (CERCLA) in an attempt to remedy environmental damage caused by hazardous substance sites. CERCLA, commonly called "Superfund", makes owners and operators of hazardous substance facilities liable for cleanup costs. CERCLA expressly excludes from this obligation anyone "who, without participating in the management of a ... facility, holds indicia of ownership primarily to protect his security interest in the ... facility." 42 U.S.A. § 9601(20)(A). Notwithstanding this provision, mortgagees, particularly those who take possession of a hazardous substance site upon default or acquire such a site at foreclosure or by deed-in-lieu of foreclosure, face potential liability for cleanup costs as an owner or operator under CERCLA.

In 1996, Congress amended CERCLA to clarify and restrict the meaning of "participating in the management of a ... facility" and to limit the risk of liability for foreclosing mortgagees. Moreover, Congress provided that an Environmental Protection Agency final rule circumscribing lender liability, previously invalidated by court decision, "shall be deemed to have been validly issued.... " Pub. L. No. 104–208 §§ 2502, 2504. Even with these measures in place, it is not uncommon for commercial mortgage lenders to arrange appropriate environmental insurance coverage.

7. Housing and Economic Recovery Act of 2008

Congress assembled the Housing and Economic Recovery Act of 2008 (Pub. L. No. 110–289) (HERA) to reinforce the destabilized housing/mortgage market in sundry ways. *See* pp. 18–19 (introducing sources of real estate financing); Ch. 10, p. 227 (noting response to 2007–2008 foreclosure escalation). Although much of this multifaceted measure deals with matters beyond this volume's purview, certain of HERA's components deserve mention.

The portion of HERA known as the Federal Housing Finance Regulatory Reform Act of 2008 undergirds and further regulates Fannie Mae and Freddie Mac. *See* pp. 37–39 (analyzing secondary mortgage market support institutions). This part of HERA also contains the HOPE for Homeowners Act of 2008, which sets up a government (FHA) insurance plan for "refinanced eligible mortgage(s)," and the Secure and Fair Enforcement for (S.A.F.E.) Mortgage Licensing Act of 2008, which creates a licensure scheme for parties who fit the category of "loan originator" of a "residential mortgage loan." See pp. 35–37 (discussing mortgage insurance and guaranty programs). In addition, HERA includes a cluster of "foreclosure prevention" initiatives, such as the FHA Modernization Act of 2008, which deals with FHA mortgage insurance, and the Mortgage Disclosure Improvement Act of 2008, which concerns Truth in Lending. *See* pp. 35–37 (discussing mortgage insurance and guaranty programs); pp. 40–42 (considering Truth in Lending). HERA concludes with the Housing Assistance Tax Act of 2008.

8. Emergency Economic Stabilization Act of 2008

The Emergency Economic Stabilization Act of 2008 (Pub. L. No. 110–343, Div. A) (EESA) authorizes the federal government to become directly involved in the secondary mortgage market through purchasing "troubled" mortgages and mortgage-backed securities from "financial institution(s)." Seller-institutions are required to grant the federal government stock acquisition rights. The Department of the Treasury is responsible for administering this bailout venture. EESA directs the federal government to strive to avert foreclosure of the residential mortgages and mortgage-backed securities it purchases.

Soon after the enactment of EESA, the federal government adjusted its bailout tactics. It rapidly crafted a stock purchase scheme designed to supply financial institutions with capital straightaway. Additional forms of federal government financial support also are part of this revised bailout endeavor.

9. Future Involvement

Given the unsettled state of the housing/mortgage market in late 2008, further federal government involvement in the real estate financing process may take place in the relatively near future. What will transpire in this regard, of course, remains to be seen.

VIII. PREDATORY LENDING

Certain mortgage lenders have made subprime mortgage loans (*see* p. 25) to financially insecure homeowners on extremely harsh, exceedingly costly terms and have done so in a deceitful manner. Existing federal statutory/regulatory schemes, particularly Truth in Lending (*see* pp. 40–42), provide ways to address such predatory lending activity. It is worth noting in this respect that the Truth in

Lending Act substantially removes the possibility of obtaining holder-in-due-course protection under UCC Article 3 for assignees of closed-end home equity loans that bear a high interest/fee rate. *See* Ch. 7, pp. 137–141 (analyzing defenses available against assignees). Nonetheless, some state legislatures have enacted measures specifically designed to deter predatory lending by limiting or barring the use of particular mortgage loan provisions and lending practices. Federal preemption via statute and regulation, however, has lessened the impact of these state legislative efforts to protect mortgagors. *See* Ch. 12, pp. 237–240 (discussing federal preemption).

CHAPTER 3

REAL ESTATE FINANCING DEVICES

I. MORTGAGE

The mortgage is the most common means of effectuating real estate financing. It is both relatively uncomplicated and flexible; most states have a statutory mortgage form that may be expanded as the parties desire. In addition, because the mortgage is a time-tested financing device, the rights and obligations of the parties are generally well established within each state. *See* Ch. 1, pp. 1–10 (discussing mortgage concept, historical development of mortgage, and mortgage theories).

A. PURCHASE MONEY MORTGAGE

The purchase money mortgage is an important mortgage species. It has been traditionally defined as a mortgage taken by the seller of real estate to secure payment of part of the purchase price. A mortgage given a third party lender as security for a loan used to acquire the mortgaged property is now also generally considered to be a purchase money mortgage.

Illustration: O contracts to sell O's house to MR for $100,000. O conveys the house to MR. MR pays O $10,000 in cash and gives O a promissory note for $90,000 secured by a mortgage on the house. The mortgage is a traditional purchase money mortgage.

Illustration: O contracts to sell O's farm to MR for $80,000. MR has only $20,000 cash, so MR obtains a $60,000 loan from ME. MR uses the cash and the loan proceeds to pay O for the farm. O conveys the farm to MR who immediately executes a mortgage on the farm to ME to secure repayment of the loan. The mortgage is generally considered a purchase money mortgage.

It is necessary to identify the purchase money mortgage for two reasons: (1) it is the type of mortgage transaction with which the home-buying public is most familiar; and (2) it receives a preferred lien priority position. *See* Ch. 9, pp. 189–190 (analyzing priority of purchase money mortgages).

B. TAX CONSIDERATIONS

A thorough examination of the tax consequences of a mortgage transaction is beyond the scope of this book. However, the significance of federal income tax considerations in real estate finance at least should be mentioned. As a general rule, the mortgagor may take an income tax deduction for interest paid on the mortgage loan, and the mortgagee must report the interest received as income. That is about as far as it goes in most residential mortgage transactions. In commercial situations, however, tax matters are often of paramount concern. Indeed, certain financing devices discussed in this chapter were developed in large part as vehicles for tax planning. Given these circumstances, it is imperative that one entering any real estate financing transaction ascertain its tax consequences at the outset, especially in this era of constant tax reform. *See* Ch. 2, p. 49 (noting Housing Assistance Tax Act of 2008).

II. DEED OF TRUST

The deed of trust is a particular kind of mortgage used in many jurisdictions. It is a tripartite arrangement in which a landowner-borrower (mortgagor) transfers an interest in land to a trustee as security for the repayment of a loan or the performance of another obligation owed a lender (mortgagee). See Ch. 1, pp. 1–2 (defining and describing mortgages). The chief practical distinction between the deed of trust and the standard mortgage is the manner of enforcement available if the borrower fails to repay the underlying obligation. The deed of trust provides for foreclosure by power of sale; the standard mortgage may or may not do so. Indeed, the deed of trust is popular in most states in which out-of-court sale is the prevalent method of foreclosure. *See* Ch. 1, pp. 7–8 & Ch. 10, pp. 217–222 (discussing foreclosure by power of sale).

The deed of trust is generally treated as a mortgage with a power-of-sale provision. The principles of mortgage law discussed in this book, therefore, generally govern the deed of trust.

III. EQUITABLE MORTGAGES

An equitable mortgage arises whenever a court finds that an apparent non-security transaction is in reality a security arrangement. Many situations exist in which this may occur. Thus the maxim: "If a transaction resolves itself into a security, whatever may be its form and whatever name the parties may choose to give it, it is, in equity, a mortgage." Those transactions that commonly spawn equitable mortgages are treated in this section.

A. ABSOLUTE DEED GIVEN AS SECURITY

A lender occasionally will require a borrower to convey property to the lender upon the understanding that the lender will hold title as security for the debt. This type of transaction is used by some lenders in an attempt to eliminate the debtor's equity of redemption and thereby avoid foreclosure. *See* Ch. 1, p. 5 (discussing preservation/clogging equity of redemption). If, however, the debtor can prove that a deed absolute on its face was intended as a security device, courts will find that an equitable mortgage was created and give the debtor an equity of redemption. Given the robust public policy against irredeemable mortgages, courts generally do not consider the parol evidence rule and the Statute of Frauds to be obstacles to this result.

The problem of proof is, however, a difficult matter. The key is the intention of the parties, a question upon which direct testimony is invariably at odds. The courts, therefore, look to several objective factors that include: the parties' prior negotiations, their relative bargaining positions, the adequacy of consideration, and who is in possession of the property. Courts usually require clear and convincing evidence of intent to create a security arrangement.

> *Illustration*: O, a landowner who desperately needs money, asks L for a mortgage loan. L offers to give O $30,000 if O will deed O's land worth $50,000 to L. O agrees upon the condition O can continue to occupy the property without paying rent. The transaction is consummated. One year later O tenders $30,000 plus interest to L and requests a deed to the property. L refuses, claiming complete ownership. O's financial difficulty, O's request for a loan, the amount O received compared to the value of the property, and O's continued possession indicate that the parties intended the absolute deed as security for a loan. The transaction, therefore, constitutes an equitable mortgage, and O can redeem the land by paying the debt.

B. CONDITIONAL SALE

The conditional sale consists of an absolute deed coupled with an option or contract to repurchase. Again the issue is whether the transaction was intended as a security device. The same evidentiary factors considered in conjunction with the absolute deed are relevant here, but certain courts are more receptive to claims that a conditional sale arrangement was crafted for security purposes.

Illustration: O, owner of a house worth $100,000, asks L for a mortgage loan. L requires and receives a deed to the house. L gives O $60,000, and the parties enter a contract in which O agrees to repurchase the house for $70,000 within one year. The character of the negotiations between O and L, the inadequacy of consideration, and O's obligation to repurchase indicate that this conditional sale was intended as a security transaction. Even if O fails to repurchase within the time period specified, courts will view the arrangement as an equitable mortgage and grant O an equity of redemption that L can cutoff only by foreclosure.

C.   NEGATIVE PLEDGE

A lender may require a borrower to agree not to encumber or convey certain of the borrower's realty until a specified loan is repaid. This type of transaction is called a negative pledge. It has been employed when the property in question is already encumbered and the lender either legally cannot take a second mortgage or chooses not to do so as a matter of customer relations. A negative pledge also has been utilized by lenders who, for local procedural reasons, wish to have the alternative of selecting between secured and unsecured creditor status depending upon which position is more advantageous from a debt collection standpoint.

The generally accepted view is that a negative pledge does not create an equitable mortgage. The affirmative intent to create a security interest cannot reasonably be inferred from a negative promise. There is, however, some authority to the contrary.

Illustration: O owns a house. O obtains a loan from Bank. Bank does not take a mortgage on O's house, but wants O to retain the house free from other liens so that O's general financial position is not weakened. Consequently, Bank makes the loan upon the condition that O not convey or further encumber the house until the loan is repaid. If O conveys or further encumbers the house, Bank may have the right to declare its entire loan due, but it has no lien to foreclose. Courts generally refuse to impose an equitable mortgage in Bank's favor on the ground there was no intent to create a security device. *But see* Coast Bank v. Minderhout, 38 Cal.Rptr. 505 (Cal. 1964) (holding that under existing circumstances equitable mortgage arose from negative pledge).

D. VENDOR'S AND VENDEE'S LIENS

Breach of a real estate contract may give rise to a lien in favor of either the vendor or the vendee as equity requires. An equitable lien generally may be imposed for the benefit of a vendor who passed legal title to the vendee, but did not receive the entire purchase price. In some states, however, the vendor's lien is not recognized unless it was expressly reserved. An equitable lien also may be imposed in favor of a vendee who paid part of the purchase price, but did not receive title because the vendor breached the contract. In either case, the lien is unlike the other types of equitable mortgages discussed in this section in that it arises by operation of law to prevent injustice, not by virtue of the judicially determined intent of the parties.

Illustration: S owns a parcel of land. S enters a binding real estate contract to convey the land to P for consideration of $10,000 in cash and a $5,000 promissory note payable thirty days after closing. P gives S the cash and the note; S deeds the land to P. At the end of thirty days, P fails to pay the note. In most states, S receives a $5,000 equitable vendor's lien on the land. In some jurisdictions, however, S does not receive a lien unless it was expressly reserved.

Illustration: S owns a parcel of land. S enters a binding real estate contract to convey the land to P. P makes a $3,000 down payment. S breaches the contract by not having a marketable title as agreed. P has a $3,000 equitable vendee's lien on the property.

IV. INSTALLMENT LAND CONTRACT

A. TRADITIONAL CONTRACT APPROACH

In a country where buying on credit is a way of life, it is to be expected that a financing device providing for the long-term installment purchase of land would be developed. The installment land contract, referred to in some states as a contract for deed, fits the bill. It gives the purchaser possession of the land immediately, but allows the purchaser to pay the sale price in monthly installments over a number of years. The seller, on the other hand, is not obligated to convey legal title until all payments have been made. Moreover, the installment land contract features a forfeiture provision to the effect that upon default the seller may recover possession, keep payments received as liquidated damages, and retain title free from any rights the purchaser had under the contract. Note that this type of agreement for the sale of land differs markedly from the standard real estate contract, which establishes the rights of the parties pending a relatively expeditious transfer of title.

Because the parties to an installment land contract are in essentially the same situation as a mortgagor and a mortgagee, one might logically conclude that the forfeiture provision is really an illegal attempt to clog the purchaser's equity of redemption. *See* Ch. 1, p. 5 (discussing preservation/clogging equity of redemption). This conclusion would be correct if courts applied mortgage law to this financing device. The installment land contract, however, developed under contract law, where freedom of contract was the guiding principle. For this reason, the installment land contract was enforced as written, forfeiture provision and all.

Treatment of the installment land contract as a contract, not a mortgage, caused it to become a popular means of real estate financing. It remains a viable arrangement in many areas of the country. Most jurisdictions still recognize the traditional contract approach, at least in limited circumstances.

Under the traditional view, the installment land contract seller enjoys the right of forfeiture—the authority to repossess the land upon default and to keep all payments made. Foreclosure of the purchaser's interest is not required. In addition, the seller obtains a tax advantage by spreading any capital gain over the term of the contract. (The seller generally may receive the same tax treatment by providing purchase-money-mortgage financing.) Purchasers, undeterred by the possibility of forfeiture, enter installment land contracts primarily because a low down-payment is required and many costs associated with mortgage financing are avoided.

Illustration: S owns land that P desires to purchase. Because mortgage-financing funds are scarce and P cannot make a large down-payment, P is unable to obtain a purchase money mortgage loan from an institutional lender. S and P, therefore, enter an installment land contract that provides for a twenty-year term with equal monthly payments of $100. P takes possession and makes payments for fifteen years. Because P is ill and out of work, P misses the first two payments in the sixteenth year. S declares forfeiture. Under the traditional contract approach, S can terminate P's interest, regain possession, and keep the payments P made ($18,000 out of the total $24,000 contract price).

B.　PROTECTING PURCHASER

There is a strong judicial and legislative trend to devise methods of protecting the purchaser from the potential severity of the traditional contract approach to installment land contracts. Protection afforded purchasers has taken a variety of forms. In some jurisdictions, more than one protective method is employed.

1.　Period-of-Grace Statutes

In certain states, statutes give the purchaser a specified amount of time to cure default before forfeiture can occur. Under these period-of-grace statutes, the seller typically is required to follow specific procedures for notifying the purchaser and terminating the purchaser's interest.

2.　Compelling Equities View

Courts in a substantial number of states have demonstrated a willingness to examine individual installment land contracts to determine whether forfeiture is appropriate under the circumstances.

This approach has been labeled the compelling equities view because forfeiture will be enforced unless the purchaser can establish reasons why it would be unjust to do so. In order to decide the appropriateness of the forfeiture in question, courts following the compelling equities view inquire into such matters as the extent of the default, the reason for default, and particularly the forfeiture involved in comparison to the contract price.

Illustration: Assume the same facts as in the immediately preceding illustration. The default was slight, of recent origin, and not willful. Further, the amount to be forfeited was the lion's share (3/4s) of the contract price. Courts in states following the compelling equities view, therefore, would not enforce the forfeiture as written. The form of relief might vary; reinstating the contract upon the payment of the overdue installments, imposing a period of grace before forfeiture, or requiring foreclosure of P's interest are three likely possibilities.

3.   Equitable Mortgage View

A few states recognize the installment land contract as a disguised mortgage and give purchasers an equity of redemption after default. This equitable mortgage view is significantly different from the compelling equities approach. All defaulting purchasers, not just those with substantial equities, are entitled to a foreclosure sale of their interest in the property.

4. Restitution

In some jurisdictions, the courts give defaulting purchasers restitution, the right to recover payments made under the installment land contract to the extent the payments exceed the seller's actual damages.

5. Waiver

Courts everywhere may employ the doctrine of waiver to grant relief to an installment land contract purchaser. A seller who has accepted late payments may be estopped to declare a forfeiture unless the seller gives reasonable notice of the intent to assert the seller's contract rights in future cases of default.

C. ENCUMBERING PURCHASER'S INTEREST

The purchaser under an installment land contract holds an interest in the land that may be encumbered. *See* Ch. 5, pp. 102–103 (discussing mortgageable interests). If the installment land contract purchaser mortgages the purchaser's interest and then defaults on the underlying installment land contract, controversy often arises between the seller and the mortgagee. Conflict centers on two issues. First, must the seller notify the mortgagee before terminating the purchaser's interest? Second, what are the mortgagee's rights after the purchaser's default?

With respect to the first issue, the general rule is that the mortgagee is entitled to notice of the impending termination of the purchaser's interest only if the seller has received notice of the mortgagee's encumbrance. Authority is split, however, as to when the seller is on notice of the mortgagee's interest. Some courts hold that the seller must have actual notice of the mortgage. These courts reason that recordation of the mortgage is not sufficient notice to the seller because recording statutes are designed to impart notice to subsequent purchasers, not prior interest holders. Other courts find that the seller need only have constructive notice of the mortgage. These courts conclude that recordation of the mortgage imparts such notice to the seller because the seller should check the records before extinguishing another's interest. This latter approach is closely analogous to the requirements imposed on a senior mortgagee who seeks to foreclose junior interest holders. *See* Ch. 10, pp. 211–213 (discussing parties defendant in judicial foreclosure).

Assuming that the mortgagee is entitled to notice of the impending termination of the purchaser's interest, a question arises concerning the mortgagee's rights in the land. In a few states, the mortgagee apparently is permitted to pay the seller the balance of the contract price and take title to the property. This approach, however, unjustly enriches the mortgagee to the extent the value of the land exceeds the total amount remaining unpaid on the installment land contract and the mortgage. Courts in other jurisdictions treat the mortgagee as a second lienor of the fee and the seller as a first lienor.

In these states, the mortgagee, therefore, may either: (1) pay off the seller and be subrogated to the seller's rights, thus becoming the holder of both the first and second liens on the property, or (2) force a sale of the property and satisfy the mortgage lien out of the sale proceeds that remain after the vendor's lien is satisfied. *See* Ch. 8, pp. 179–182 (discussing equity of redemption); Ch. 10, p. 216 (treating distribution of foreclosure sale proceeds). Under either alternative, the mortgagee is entitled to recover the value of its lien, but no more. This treatment of the seller and mortgagee as first and second lienors is consistent with the overall movement toward treating installment land contracts as mortgages and, hence, can be expected to gain support.

D.   ENCUMBERING SELLER'S INTEREST

The installment land contract seller also holds an interest in the property that may be encumbered. *See* Ch. 5, pp. 102–103 (discussing mortgageable interests). This is commonly accomplished by the seller executing, as security for a loan, both an assignment of the right to receive payments under the contract and a mortgage on, or a conveyance of, the legal title that the seller retains. Sometimes an installment land contract seller pledges as security just the right to payments. Holders of these various kinds of security interests may insure priority over the seller's future lien creditors and bankruptcy trustee by filing a financing statement under Article 9 of the Uniform Commercial Code (UCC). *See* UCC

§ 9–308(e). Recording in the land records is neither required nor adequate to achieve this purpose.

V. LEASE

A. VARIETIES

The lease plays an important part in real estate finance, particularly in the area of commercial development. Leases may be used in a variety of ways, frequently in conjunction with another financing device.

1. Ground Lease

A ground lease is a long-term lease employed to acquire raw land for commercial development. Its principal advantages to the lessee over outright purchase are that little or no "up-front" capital is needed and rental payments are tax deductible. The ground lease and the improvements to be constructed on the property are then mortgaged to finance development. The concept of the leasehold mortgage is discussed later in this chapter. *See* pp. 69–71.

Illustration: D desires to develop a shopping center on O's unimproved land. D and O enter a ground lease for a sixty-year term. Other lease provisions are as follows: D will complete the shopping center within a certain time period; ground rent is not payable until the center is completed; D must pay all taxes, utilities, insurance, and maintenance on the property; and all improvements belong to D until the term of the ground lease expires when they go with the land to O. D then obtains mortgage financing for the project. As indicated in this illustration, the tenant under a typical ground lease is responsible for taxes, insurance, and maintenance. When a lease contains a provision of this type it is said to be a "net" lease because the rental income to the lessor is not reduced by payment of operating expenses.

2. Space Lease

The financial success of many developments depends upon the developer's ability to rent the store, apartment, or office space in the project. Space leases play such a significant role in the success of shopping centers and office buildings that permanent mortgage lenders generally require the developer to obtain space lease commitments from a number of substantial tenants before construction begins.

3. Acquisition Lease

In many instances a business will utilize a long-term lease to acquire improved commercial property for expansion of its operations. Because this type of lease is employed as an alternative to the purchase or construction of new facilities, it is called an acquisition lease in these materials.

The attractions of an acquisition lease to the lessee are much the same as that of a ground lease: small front-end cash outlay and tax-deductible rental payments. These attractions, however, are somewhat stronger in the case of an acquisition lease because of the generally higher value of the lease-hold being acquired.

An acquisition lease is usually a "net" lease and often contains an escalator clause that adjusts the amount of rent to keep pace with inflation. The Consumer Price Index maintained by the Department of Labor is an economic indicator frequently used to accomplish this result. An acquisition lease, of course, is not the only type of lease in which escalator clauses are found.

B.   LEASEHOLD MORTGAGE

A lessee may mortgage the leasehold estate. *See* Ch. 5, pp. 102–103 (considering mortgageable interests). Although the discussion of mortgage law in this book concerns fee mortgages, it is generally applicable to leasehold mortgages. However, additional issues arise when a mortgagee accepts a leasehold as security.

1.   Nature of Security

Leasehold mortgage financing involves an inherent drawback; the mortgagee's security interest is subject to the rights of the lessor-owner. Consequently, many mortgagees will not make a leasehold mortgage loan unless the lessor subordinates the fee to the mortgage. *See* Ch. 9, p. 195 (discussing subordination of fee to leasehold mortgage). The lessor may be hesitant to do so because subordination impairs the lessor's ability to borrow on the reversion and subjects the fee to sale upon the lessee's

default. Nevertheless, important financial factors
may cause the lessor to take this step. Subordination of the fee usually enables the lessee to obtain
financing that is otherwise unavailable. Hence, the
lessor may demand higher rent and receive property
of greater value at the end of the lease term.

2.   Lease Provisions

When the lease and leasehold mortgage are successive steps in one financing package, the lease is
drafted to meet the requirements of the proposed
mortgagee. If, however, the lease predates the mortgage negotiations, it usually is amended as specified
by the mortgagee. In either case, leasehold mortgage financing presents unique problems. The areas
of greatest concern to the mortgagee are treated in
the following subsections of this chapter. Discussion
of many other matters important to the mortgagee
is outside the purview of this work.

a.   *Term*

The lease term should be at least as long as the
mortgage term; otherwise the security will cease to
exist before the mortgage debt is paid.

b.   *Transfer*

As a general rule, the lessee may encumber, assign, and sublet the leasehold unless the lease or a
statute provides otherwise. The lessee's ability to
encumber the estate is obviously essential to the
creation of a leasehold mortgage. The lease, therefore, should not limit the lessee's rights in this

regard and preferably should specifically permit the lessee to mortgage the leasehold. Also, because the mortgagee may acquire the leasehold upon foreclosure, the lease should not impose restrictions on assignment or subleasing, at least as against the mortgagee.

c. Default

Termination of the lease extinguishes the leasehold mortgage. Thus, the mortgagee usually requires that it receive notice of and the right to cure the tenant's defaults under the lease.

C. SALE AND LEASEBACK

The lease also constitutes part of an important financing vehicle known as the sale and leaseback. This financing technique is enormously complex in its many variations. The scope of this book permits presentation of only the basic concept.

A typical sale and leaseback is structured as follows: the owner of improved commercial property sells it to an investor who leases the property right back to the seller on a long-term, "net" basis. The reasons behind this rather puzzling transaction lie in the intricacies of business finance and federal income tax law.

The essential business finance factors are not difficult to comprehend. The owner of the property is able to obtain more capital from the sale and leaseback arrangement than from mortgage financing. Although mortgage loans usually are subject to loan-to-value limits, the sale aspect of the sale and leaseback may produce almost 100% of current fair market value. Investors are willing to provide such financing because they generally receive a higher rate of return from a sale and leaseback than from a mortgage loan. Furthermore, the return is not limited by usury statutes, which apply only to loan transactions.

The general tax ramifications of a sale and lease-back are also easily understood. The seller-lessee realizes a capital gain or loss on the sale of the property and may deduct all rent paid. (Recall that only the interest portion of mortgage loan payments may be deducted.) The investor-lessor receives rental income, but may claim depreciation deductions on the property.

The elaborate plans of the parties, however, will collapse if the transaction is found to be a security arrangement rather than a genuine sale and lease-back. Factors that tend to indicate that the transaction is really a disguised mortgage are similar to those noted in the section of this chapter on equitable mortgages. *See* pp. 55–57 (discussing absolute deed given as security and conditional sale). They include the following: the seller-lessee is financially embarrassed; the parties have not dealt at arm's length; the sale price is inadequate; the transaction, if a mortgage loan, would be usurious; and the seller-lessee is given an option to purchase for a nominal amount.

In the event the transaction is found to be a hidden security arrangement instead of a legitimate sale and leaseback, disastrous consequences may result. First, the parties must readjust their tax positions to reflect reality and pay any resulting tax deficiencies. Second, a question of usury may arise. Third, upon default the investor must terminate the "lessee's" interest in the property by utilizing foreclosure procedures, rather than by declaring forfeiture under the lease and seeking summary eviction.

VI.   MEZZANINE LOAN

Although not a mortgage arrangement itself, a mezzanine loan may be linked with mortgage financing. A lending institution may make a loan secured by equity in an entity that is the remote owner of mortgaged realty via its ownership of the mortgagor. Such a mezzanine loan, situated higher than the equity and lower than the mortgage in general terms of priority, has the potential of producing more financing than is possible through a second mortgage loan. *See* Ch. 2, pp. 28–34 (analyzing secondary financing).

CHAPTER 4

UNDERLYING OBLIGATION

I. NECESSITY FOR UNDERLYING OBLIGATION

A mortgage is only security. It cannot exist without an underlying obligation. There is, however, no requirement that the mortgagor or anyone else be personally liable on the obligation. A mortgage transaction in which no person or institution has liability is known as a "nonrecourse" or "in rem" mortgage loan.

Illustration: MR executes a promissory note and a mortgage to ME. The note contains a provision that MR shall have no personal responsibility to pay the note and that ME's only remedy in event of default is to foreclose. The mortgage is valid because a "real" obligation supports it.

Illustration: MR executes a promissory note and a mortgage to ME. MR conveys the mortgaged property to GE "subject to" the mortgage. GE does not assume personal responsibility to pay the note. ME then releases MR from liability, but retains its rights under the mortgage. The mortgage continues unaffected by this transaction even though no one is personally liable on the note.

II. FORM OF OBLIGATION

A mortgage may secure any obligation that has an ascertainable monetary value. A court upon foreclosure must be able to determine the amount of the lien in order to distribute the sale proceeds properly. *See* Ch. 10, p. 216 (discussing distribution of proceeds).

Illustration: ME owns ten acres of land and agrees to sell two acres to MR upon the condition that MR build a sewer to service the entire original tract. MR pays the full purchase price and executes a mortgage to ME to secure the required promise. The mortgage indeed secures the promise to build the sewer. The obligation is one that can be reduced to a money equivalent. *See* Jeffrey Towers, Inc. v. Straus, 31 A.D.2d 319 (N.Y.App. Div.1969).

Notwithstanding the generally accepted view stated above, some authority exists for the proposition that the underlying obligation need not be quantifiable in monetary terms. *See* id. This approach has been adopted primarily with respect to mortgages given as security for a promise to provide support for an elderly grantor-mortgagee.

The underlying obligation may be embodied in the mortgage itself, but is usually evidenced by a separate promissory note. The promissory note may be negotiable. *See* UCC § 3–104(a). A statement in the instrument that it is secured by a mortgage does not destroy its negotiability. *See* UCC § 3–106(a). The note's negotiability is likewise unimpaired by its reference to the mortgage for rights as to prepayment or acceleration. *See* UCC § 3–106(b). If, however, the note incorporates terms of the mortgage for other purposes, it becomes a conditional promise and is thereby rendered nonnegotiable.

III. DESCRIPTION OF OBLIGATION

As between the mortgagor and the mortgagee, it is prudent, but not necessary, to describe the underlying obligation in the mortgage. A description of the obligation, however, is necessary to protect the mortgagee against subsequent purchasers and lienors. Although authorities disagree regarding what information is required to impart adequate notice of the obligation to third parties, the description should specify the obligation's form, amount, interest rate, execution date, and maturity date. The mortgagee, of course, must also record the mortgage to preserve its priority. *See* Ch. 9, pp. 186–187 (discussing recording statutes).

IV. FUTURE ADVANCES
A. THE BASIC CONCEPT

A mortgage may secure the repayment of funds that the mortgagee advances to the mortgagor in the future. In fact, many commonly used mortgage forms contain a future advances clause. Home equity loans, for example, sometimes include such a provision. *See* Ch. 2, pp. 30–31 (discussing mortgagor's "equity" and home equity loan concept). The future advances clause also is an integral part of construction loan mortgages under which the lender advances funds as construction on the mortgaged property progresses.

A mortgage that covers future advances constitutes an executory agreement by the mortgagor that the mortgaged property stands as security for all funds advanced by the mortgagee. The arrangement is essentially one transaction, not a series of independent loans. It is specifically so designed for the convenience and economic advantage of the parties. Thus, the lien of a mortgage for future advances arises as at the date of the execution of the mortgage, not when advances are made.

B.   METHODS OF SECURING FUTURE ADVANCES

The parties generally provide for coverage of future advances by drafting the mortgage in either of two ways. One technique is to specify a present loan amount in excess of funds actually advanced. A second approach is to state the amount of the current debt and then provide that the mortgage secures future advances, with or without limit on the total amount secured. Both methods have been upheld by the courts, but the second alternative is more common.

C. OBLIGATORY/OPTIONAL DISTINCTION

A mortgagee who holds a properly recorded mortgage for future advances receives priority over parties who subsequently acquire an interest in the mortgaged property. *See* Ch. 9, pp. 186–187 (discussing recording statutes). Courts, however, sometimes limit the priority of a mortgage for future advances in order to preserve the marketability of the mortgaged property for subsequent encumbrance or sale. The necessity for limitation depends in large part upon whether the future advance is obligatory or optional.

1. Obligatory Future Advances

If a mortgagee is contractually obligated to make future advances, the lien for each advance has priority over any encumbrance that attaches to the property subsequent to the execution of the mortgage. This rule applies even when the mortgagee makes an advance with knowledge of an encumbrance that arose in the interim between the execution of the mortgage and the advance. No policy reason exists to change the principle that priority for future advances dates from the day the mortgage was executed. Because the mortgagor has the right to additional future advances, the mortgagor is not prejudiced by the fact that secondary financing on the property is probably unavailable from another lender.

Illustration: MR and ME enter a construction loan agreement that ME will advance funds up to a total of $1,000,000 as construction on the mortgaged property progresses. MR executes a $1,000,000 promissory note and a mortgage to ME who records the mortgage. ME advances $500,000 as construction progresses in accordance with the agreement. At that point, MR borrows $200,000 from X and gives X a $200,000 promissory note secured by a mortgage on the same property. X records. ME knows of this lien, but because MR fully complies with the construction loan agreement, ME advances the remaining $500,000. ME has a first lien for $1,000,000 because it was obligated to advance the entire loan amount. X has a second lien for $200,000.

2. Optional Future Advances

Many mortgages for future advances provide that future advances are optional with the mortgagee. Mortgages for optional future advances are sometimes referred to as open-end mortgages.

a. Priority Problems

Controversy often arises regarding the priority of optional advances over encumbrances that attach to the mortgaged property following the execution of the mortgage. The outcome depends upon which of three possible fact patterns is presented: (1) The lien for optional future advances made *before* the attachment of a subsequent encumbrance clearly has priority under the fundamental principle of "prior in time, prior in right." *See* Ch. 9, pp. 186–187 (discussing recording statutes). (2) The lien for optional future advances made *after* the attachment of a subsequent encumbrance and *without notice* of that encumbrance also has priority on the theory that it arose at the date that the mortgage for future advances was executed. (3) The lien for optional future advances made *with notice* of the attachment of a subsequent encumbrance is generally postponed to the lien of the intervening encumbrance on the ground that the marketability of the mortgagor's land for subsequent encumbrance or sale would otherwise be virtually destroyed. If other lenders were unable to ensure the priority of their encumbrances over the lien of later optional future advances, they certainly would not make mortgage loans on the property. The mortgagor then would be left to the whim of the original mortgagee for additional financing. Likewise, it is improbable that potential purchasers would be willing to acquire the property subject to a mortgage arrangement that put the original mortgagee in such a dominant position.

b.   *Notice Issue*

The "notice" limitation on the priority of optional future advances is clouded by disagreement over the type of notice required. There are two views on the subject. The generally accepted view is that the lien of an optional future advance loses priority to the lien of an intervening encumbrance only if the mortgagee has actual notice of the encumbrance when it makes the advance. Some states, however, postpone the lien of an optional future advance to the lien of an intervening encumbrance when the mortgagee has either actual or constructive notice of the encumbrance. In these jurisdictions, recording the encumbrance imparts constructive notice of its existence to the mortgagee. This approach, however, is inconsistent with established legal principles. Recording systems are designed to work prospectively only; subsequent purchasers, not prior interest holders, receive constructive notice of a recorded document. *See* Ch. 9, pp. 186–187 (discussing recording statutes). A mortgagee who makes optional future advances after an intervening encumbrance is recorded can be considered a subsequent purchaser only if the future advance is viewed as a separate loan. This is, of course, contrary to the fundamental notion that the lien for future advances arises at the date of the execution of the mortgage, not when the advance is made.

Illustration: MR borrows $20,000 from ME and gives ME a $20,000 promissory note and a mortgage. The mortgage contains an optional future advances clause and provides for a maximum total indebtedness of $30,000. ME records. MR then borrows $5,000 from X and gives X a $5,000 promissory note secured by a mortgage on the same property. X records. MR next borrows an additional $10,000 from ME under the optional future advances clause in the original mortgage. The generally accepted view is that ME has a first lien for $30,000 unless it had actual notice of X's lien at the time it made the future advance. In some jurisdictions, however, ME's lien for the

future advance is postponed in priority to X's lien
on the ground that ME was on constructive notice of X's encumbrance. In these states, ME has
a first lien for $20,000, X has a second lien for
$5,000, and ME has a third lien for $10,000.

D.   OBLIGATORY/OPTIONAL
DISTINCTION REJECTED
BY STATUTE

Certain state legislatures have enacted statutes
eliminating the distinction between obligatory and
optional future advances with respect to various
mortgage loan transactions. In these jurisdictions,
the lien of all future advances dates from the execution of a mortgage covered by the statute even if the
mortgagee makes the advance with actual knowledge of an intervening encumbrance. In other
words, obligatory and optional advances are treated
the same; each takes priority over intervening encumbrances. Almost all of the statutes that produce
this result, however, require that the mortgage
specify the total amount to be secured. Moreover,
some of these legislative measures allow the mortgagor to restrict the operation of a future advances
clause to funds already disbursed by filing a prescribed notice.

E.   CONSTRUCTION LENDER'S
DILEMMA

The distinction between obligatory and optional
future advances for priority purposes has been se-

verely criticized by construction lenders on the ground that its application to advances made under a construction loan mortgage often produces inequitable results. Because the construction lender is obligated to make advances as construction progresses, it receives first lien priority for all advances when the project is completed according to plan. Problems arise, however, when construction does not progress smoothly and the borrower-developer defaults. Construction loan documents typically give the lender the right to stop advancing funds upon the mortgagor's default. Hence, any advances made thereafter are optional and may lose priority to intervening liens. If, however, the construction lender does not make additional advances, the incomplete project probably will not be of sufficient value even to cover the amount of the lien for obligatory advances made before default.

Courts may struggle with the optional/obligatory future advance rule in this situation because completion of the project enhances the value of the security for both the construction lender and any intervening lienor. Although the hazy line dividing optional and obligatory advances gives the judiciary ample opportunity to exercise discretion, generally judges mechanistically apply the optional/obligatory rule and conclude that advances made after default are optional. A few courts, however, apparently will award the construction lender complete lien priority if the lender makes post default advances in good faith and under economic compulsion. This result, long favored by commentators, is reached by statute in those states in which the legislature has eliminated the distinction between obligatory and optional future advances.

F. DRAGNET CLAUSE

The dragnet clause is related to the future advances clause, but is broader in scope. The typical dragnet clause, sometimes referred to as an anaconda, cross-security, or omnibus clause, provides that the mortgage secures all indebtedness owed by the mortgagor to the mortgagee. Every obligation is included, regardless of whether it arose before or after the execution of the mortgage or whether it was originated or acquired by the mortgagee.

Illustration: MR executes a $2,000 unsecured promissory note to X. MR then borrows $5,000 from ME and executes a $5,000 promissory note and a mortgage to ME. The mortgage contains a dragnet clause. ME purchases the unsecured note from X at a discount for $1,500. ME now has a $7,000 lien on the mortgage property because both notes are fully secured by the mortgage.

Because a dragnet clause can be used to expand the amount of a lien far beyond the mortgagor's expectations, its scope has been limited by both judicial decision and state legislative action. Numerous forms of limitation exist. Judicially crafted restrictions confine application of the dragnet clause to certain obligations, such as those created directly between the original parties to the mortgage, those arising after execution of the mortgage, or those consistent with the objective of the initial loan. The extent to which courts employ any of these restrictions varies among the states.

V. INTEREST
A. THE NORM

The underlying obligation normally bears interest at a fixed percentage rate per annum. The precise interest rate charged is usually dictated by money market conditions existing at the time the mortgage loan is made. But regardless of what the rate may be, it remains constant over the entire term of the loan.

A lender may increase its yield beyond the stated fixed interest rate by requiring the borrower to pay discount points at the time the loan is made. One discount point equals one percent of the loan amount.

Illustration: ME agrees to make a $100,000 thirty-year mortgage loan to MR at a 10% fixed interest rate plus two points. MR must pay $2,000 to ME at the time the loan is made. This payment increases the loan's effective yield to above 10%. The amount of the increase depends upon when the loan is paid off. The earlier the payoff, the greater the increase.

B. VARIATIONS FROM THE NORM

During periods of rampant inflation, a fixed rate of interest provides the lender with less yield than

originally projected. Consequently, mortgagees have
devised other methods to insure a satisfactory return on their investments. Lenders who employ
these variations from the norm also may charge
discount points for making the loan.

1.   Alternative Mortgage Instruments

In the 1970s and early 1980s, the Comptroller of
the Currency, the Federal Home Loan Bank Board
(today the Office of Thrift Supervision), and the
National Credit Union Administration authorized
the federally-chartered lending institutions under
their control to develop alternatives to the traditional mortgage. Moreover, the Alternative Mortgage Transaction Parity Act of 1982, 12 U.S.C.A.
§ 3801 *et seq.*, preempted state law on the subject
and enabled nonfederally-chartered institutions to
compete effectively in the residential real estate
financing marketplace by authorizing them to offer
the same alternative residential mortgage instruments available from similar federally-chartered institutions. The states had three years from the
passage of the Act to override this preemption.
Some states reinstituted local law by doing so.

As a consequence of these regulatory and legislative measures, several significant alternatives to the
traditional mortgage have been developed by institutional lenders. Those innovative instruments that
alter the standard fixed-interest-rate approach are
discussed in this section. Newly developed mortgage
formats that provide payment alternatives are
treated later in this chapter. Neither analysis is

intended to be exhaustive. Some existing alternative mortgage instruments are not mentioned, and additional variations constantly are being introduced.

a. Adjustable Rate Mortgage

Mortgage lenders now offer adjustable rate mortgages (ARMs) in which the interest rate rises and falls over the term of the loan in accordance with prevailing market conditions. The market rate of interest is gauged by a predetermined index—some recognized economic indicator reflecting changes in the cost of obtaining mortgage money in the local, regional, or national market. The parties may guard against extreme interest rate fluctuations by establishing floor and ceiling limits.

ARMs, sometimes referred to as variable rate mortgages (VRMs), may be structured in an almost infinite number of ways. Variations exist not only with respect to the index and the use of floors and ceilings, but also as to the frequency and amount of each interest rate adjustment and the way in which interest increases are paid. Moreover, an ARM may be drafted to include other flexibility features such as a graduated payment provision.

Some ARMs include another noteworthy feature. If increases in the interest rate are added to the principal obligation rather than reflected in increased monthly payments or extended maturity, the phenomenon of negative amortization may occur. That is, over time the principal balance of the loan may increase instead of decrease.

A study conducted by the Federal Home Loan Mortgage Corporation (now Freddie Mac) revealed that ARMs had achieved a prominent position in the mortgage-financing marketplace by the early 1980s. The ARM's share of the residential mortgage market has varied over the years depending upon inflation and the volatility of interest rates. During periods of moderate inflation and relative interest rate stability, ARMs tend to become less popular with borrowers.

For a time, an unsettling development in the case law made ARMs less attractive to purchasers of mortgage loans on the secondary mortgage market. Several courts concluded that ARM notes were non-negotiable on the ground the notes did not contain an obligation to pay a "sum certain." *See* UCC §§ 3–104(1)(b), 3–106 (pre–1990). Assignees of such nonnegotiable instruments are not eligible to receive the favorable treatment available under Article 3 of the UCC for assignees of negotiable instruments. *See* Ch. 7, pp. 137–147 (discussing defenses available against assignees and payment problems after assignment). Experts in the field, therefore, called for amendment of the UCC to include ARM notes within the definition of negotiable instruments. In 1990, the UCC was revised to so provide. *See* UCC § 3–112(b). Consequently, the ARM-negotiability issue has been resolved.

b.   *Price Level Adjusted Mortgage*

A mortgage format often used in other parts of the world to insulate lenders against inflation is the price level adjusted mortgage (PLAM), also known as an indexed mortgage (IM). This instrument deals with the problem of inflation by tying the outstanding principal to an economic index. Thus, the interest rate remains constant over the term of the loan, but the loan principal varies. In this sense, a PLAM is the opposite of an ARM.

An advantage of the PLAM to the mortgagor is that it bears a low interest rate because inflation need not be factored into the rate of return required by the lender. On the other hand, the PLAM's primary drawback for the borrower is that it produces negative amortization which is usually covered by increased monthly payments.

c. Shared Appreciation Mortgage

Shared appreciation mortgages (SAMs) are designed to insure mortgagees of an adequate return during inflationary times and to provide an alternative form of financing for individuals who otherwise might be unable to obtain a mortgage loan. SAMs combine aspects of the standard fixed-interest-rate mortgage with a novel type of return to the lender. Typically, SAMs bear a fixed-interest-rate well below current market rates thereby enabling a greater number of individuals to qualify for this form of financing than for standard fixed-interest-rate mortgages or ARMs. The SAM instrument also provides that the mortgagee will receive a portion (e.g., one-third) of the amount the mortgaged property appreciates in value. The lender's fractional share of the appreciation is paid when the property is sold or at the end of a certain period (e.g., ten years), whichever comes first. This share is often called contingent interest.

Although the SAM has appeal to both mortgagees and mortgagors, its use raises a myriad of issues: How does one determine the amount of appreciation? How are improvements made by the mortgagor factored into the calculation of appreciation? If the mortgagor does not sell the property before the lender's share of appreciation must be paid, will satisfactory refinancing be available? These and other questions cloud the SAM picture and lead authorities to draw differing conclusions regarding its future in the residential mortgage marketplace.

2. Buy–Down Mortgage

Mortgagees generally are willing to make below-market-interest-rate loans if they receive sufficient upfront money to offset the reduced interest rate of return. A mortgage loan made on this basis is called a "buy-down." Real estate developers and other sellers may use the buy-down technique to make their residential properties more marketable by paying an institutional lender to offer low-interest-rate financing to purchasers. In such case, the interest buy-down is typically for only a short term, such as a year or two; thereafter the interest rate returns to the market level.

3. Revenue/Equity Participation

As a hedge against inflation, mortgage lenders sometimes demand a portion of the revenue generated by the project being financed. When this occurs, the lender is said to receive contingent interest or an "equity kicker." Under such an arrangement, the lender typically is entitled to a percentage of gross income or net profits in addition to the specified interest.

Mortgagees may go even further and obtain an ownership interest in the project. Several types of such equity participations exist. The lender may become directly involved by entering a joint venture with the developer or by taking an ownership interest in the entity that controls the project. Equity participation should be distinguished from loan participation discussed earlier. *See,* Ch. 2, p. 27 (analyzing loan participation).

C.   DUE–ON–SALE CLAUSE

The due-on-sale clause is commonly used by mortgagees to avoid being tied to low yield mortgages during periods of rising interest rates. A mortgage provision of this type gives the lender the option to accelerate the underlying obligation when the mortgagor conveys the mortgaged property. As a practical matter, this enables the mortgagee either to recover its capital for reinvestment at a higher return or to obtain an additional return on the original loan by conditioning its consent to the conveyance on the payment of a transfer fee or an increased interest rate. *See* Ch. 6, pp. 123–130 (discussing due-on-sale clause).

D. USURY

The amount of interest a lender may receive is limited by state usury statutes. The provisions of these measures differ considerably with regard to: (1) the maximum legal interest rate (2) statutory exemptions, and (3) penalties for violation.

1. Rate

The maximum allowable interest rate on loans varies dramatically among the states. In many jurisdictions, different maximum rates exist for different types of borrowers. For example, there may be one rate for individuals and another higher rate for corporations.

2. Exemptions

Most usury statutes exempt certain borrowers, lenders, transactions, or a combination of the three.

a. Borrowers

Corporate borrowers are commonly exempt from usury statutes. Moreover, as previously indicated, where corporate borrowers are not exempt, they are usually permitted to pay a higher rate of interest than other borrowers. Authority is divided on the issue of whether the lender may avoid usury laws by requiring the borrower to incorporate.

b. Lenders

Banks and savings and loan associations are exempt from usury statutes in several states.

c.   Transactions

FHA insured loans are often excluded from the application of usury laws. In addition, a purchase money mortgage loan taken by a seller of real estate is exempt in many jurisdictions on the theory that a buyer and seller are in substantially equal bargaining positions. Various other transactions, such as loans for business purposes, are sometimes given exempt status.

3. Penalties

In some states, the penalty for usury is merely forfeiture of interest in excess of the legal rate. In many jurisdictions, the lender forfeits all interest. Elsewhere, the lender not only forfeits all interest, but also loses the right to recover the principal. Still other penalties exist.

4. Federal Preemption

The Depository Institutions Deregulation and Monetary Control Act of 1980 preempted several aspects of state usury law. The most significant provision for real estate financing purposes is that portion of the Act which exempts most residential first mortgage loans from state interest rate limits. 12 U.S.C.A. § 1735f–7a. The Act gave the states the option to override this federal preemption within a three-year time frame. Several states did so. Thus, although the Act provides some uniformity in this area of usury law, considerable diversity still exists among the states.

VI.   MODIFICATION OF OBLIGATION

A mortgage secures an obligation, not the instrument that evidences it. A change in the form of the obligation by substitution, extension, or renewal, therefore, generally does not affect the mortgage lien. If, however, either the obligation's principal or its interest rate is increased by modification, the mortgage lien may lose priority to junior encumbrances for the amount of the increase.

VII.   DISCHARGE OF OBLIGATION AND MORTGAGE
A.   PAYMENT

As discussed previously, a mortgage merely secures an underlying obligation. *See* Ch. 1, pp. 1–3 (discussing mortgage concept). Thus, once the obligation is discharged, usually by payment, the mortgage is extinguished.

The typical modern mortgage loan is amortized over fifteen to thirty years with provision for repayment in monthly installments of principal and interest. The amount of the mortgage lien is reduced proportionately as each monthly payment is made. When the debt is paid in full, the mortgage is discharged.

Illustration: MR executes a $25,000 promissory note and a mortgage to ME. MR pays ME $15,000 on the principal of the note. The amount of the mortgage lien is reduced automatically to $10,000 notwithstanding the fact the mortgage states that it secures a $25,000 debt.

1. Payment Alternatives

Lending institutions have been authorized to offer alternatives to the traditional payment format.

a. *Graduated Payment Mortgage*

Under the graduated payment mortgage (GPM), the interest rate usually remains constant throughout the life of the loan, but monthly mortgage payments increase over several years to a specified level. Initial payments are lower than normally required, whereas later payments are abnormally high. Thus, younger homebuyers may make smaller mortgage payments in their early years of employment and larger ones as their income presumably increases. This graduated payment feature may be coupled with an adjustable interest rate.

b. *Reverse Mortgage*

The reverse mortgage allows older homeowners to borrow money on the equity in their homes. Reverse mortgages may take various forms. Under one approach, the loan proceeds are advanced to the mortgagor in monthly installments and are repaid in a lump sum at the end of a set term, when the home is sold, or at the homeowner's death.

c. *Growing Equity Mortgage*

One alternative mortgage instrument includes a fixed interest rate, but provides for increasing monthly principal payments so that the loan is repaid in fifteen years or so. It is from this feature that the instrument takes its name—growing equity mortgage (GEM).

Initial payments under a GEM are based on a twenty-five or thirty year amortization. The rate of increased principal payments is specified in the document and may be fixed at a certain percentage or tied to an economic index.

2. Balloon Loans

Many residential mortgage loans executed before the Depression were short-term "balloon" loans upon which the borrower paid only interest until maturity. If the borrower lacked sufficient funds to satisfy the debt when it fell due, the borrower was forced to refinance. This arrangement worked well as long as mortgage loans were readily available. During the Depression, however, money was in short supply, and many borrowers were unable to refinance. Consequently, numerous mortgagors lost their land through foreclosure. This situation caused the federal government to develop programs, notably FHA mortgage insurance, to encourage the use of long-term, fully-amortized mortgages.

Today, a balloon mortgage loan may be defined as one that requires a substantial payment at the end of the term to cover the unamortized loan principal. Disclosure and other aspects of balloon payment terms may be governed by regulation or statute.

3. Escrow Accounts

The mortgagor frequently is required to make monthly payments that cover not only principal and interest, but also build an escrow account from which the mortgagee may pay real estate taxes and insurance on the mortgaged property as they come due. The escrow account system originated during the Depression when many mortgagors were unable to pay real estate taxes or insurance premiums, and lenders were forced to pay these obligations in order to protect their security.

The handling of escrow account funds traditionally has been left to the mortgagee's discretion. Mortgagees commonly invest escrowed monies with their other funds and keep the resulting returns.

Mortgagors in numerous jurisdictions have instituted lawsuits, often class actions, contesting the legality of a mortgagee's decision not to pay interest on funds held in escrow. Mortgagors have sought relief on various grounds, including express trust and constructive trust theories. These suits generally have been unsuccessful. Although mortgagors occasionally have prevailed, *see, e.g.,* Buchanan v. Century Federal Savings and Loan Association of Pittsburgh, 542 A.2d 117 (Pa.Super.1988), courts usually have been unwilling to require mortgagees to account for earnings received from the investment of escrowed funds.

The mortgagors' attack on interest-free escrow accounts has achieved greater success outside the courtroom. Controversy fueled by their lawsuits has precipitated federal and state legislative action. The federal Real Estate Settlement Procedures Act limits the amount of funds that may be placed in escrow (*See* Ch. 2, p. 46), and statutes in some states require the payment of interest on these accounts.

4. Late Charges

The mortgagor is often required to pay a late charge when tardy in making monthly payments. Considerable division of opinion exists regarding whether to treat late charges as liquidated damages or as additional interest. Nonetheless, as a general proposition, courts uphold late charges calculated on a reasonable basis as nonusurious compensation for the cost of handling overdue payments. Some courts have refused to permit lenders to recover late charges on top of default interest. In many states, late charges are limited in amount or otherwise regulated by statute.

5. Default Interest

Mortgage loan documents sometimes call for an increased rate of interest post-default. *See* Ch. 8, pp. 162–164 (analyzing default). Courts typically uphold provisions for default interest, either as contractual arrangements regarding interest or as establishing liquidated damages. Nevertheless, default interest has been invalidated in certain cases as unconscionable or unreasonable. In this regard, some courts have prohibited lenders from receiving default interest along with late charges. Default interest also may be restricted by usury statutes. *See* pp. 92–93 (discussing usury).

B. PREPAYMENT

The mortgagee contracts to receive interest over the agreed term of the loan. The mortgagor, therefore, has no right to pay the underlying obligation prior to maturity unless the mortgage, the note, a local statute, or a court opinion specifically authorizes the mortgagor to do so.

Illustration: MR borrows $5,000 from ME and executes a $5,000 promissory note and a mortgage to ME. The note is due five years from the date of execution and bears interest at 12% per annum. The instruments are silent regarding prepayment. The next day MR's parents give MR $5,000. MR immediately tenders ME $5,000 to satisfy the loan. In most jurisdictions, ME may reject MR's tender and collect interest as specified in the mortgage note. In a few states, however, a statute or a court opinion gives MR the right to prepay even though MR does not have a contractual right to do so.

Residential mortgage loan documents frequently authorize prepayment without charge. Commercial mortgage documents commonly contain a provision giving the mortgagor the privilege to prepay for a fee. The fee, often called a prepayment penalty, may be calculated in various ways. Prepayment penalties usually are not included in residential mortgage loans.

Prepayment penalties generally are enforceable as reasonable compensation for lost interest and other costs. This broad proposition is, however, subject to several caveats. First, statutes in many states limit the use of prepayment penalties in residential mortgage financing. Second, Truth in Lending regulates prepayment penalties in certain residential mortgage loans. See Ch. 2, pp. 40–42 (analyzing Truth in Lending). Third, some bankruptcy decisions have curtailed or invalidated prepayment penalty provisions. Fourth, courts are reluctant to permit the lender to collect a prepayment penalty when the mortgagor is forced to pay off the loan because the lender accelerated under a general default provision or a due-on-sale clause. Involuntary payment required under such circumstances generally is not viewed as *pre*payment triggering a penalty unless the mortgage specifically so provides. In this regard, Office of Thrift Supervision regulations issued under the Garn–St. Germain Depository Institutions Act of 1982 prohibit mortgagees from charging a prepayment penalty in connection with the enforcement of a due-on-sale clause in a mortgage on a borrower-occupied residence. 12 C.F.R. § 591.5(b)(2) (2008). *See* Ch. 6, pp. 129–130 (discussing practical considerations of enforcing due-on-sale clause).

C. RELEASE OF MORTGAGE

Although the mortgage lien is automatically extinguished when the underlying obligation is satisfied, the recorded mortgage continues to cloud the mortgagor's title. The mortgagor, therefore, is entitled to a recordable mortgage release upon final payment. Mortgagees who wrongfully refuse to execute a release are subject to common law remedies and, in numerous jurisdictions, to statutory penalties as well.

D. STATUTE OF LIMITATIONS

In some states the statute of limitations on the obligation is shorter than the statute of limitations on the mortgage. *See* Ch. 10, p. 208 (discussing statute of limitations on mortgage). When the statute runs on the obligation but not the mortgage, controversy arises regarding the enforceability of the mortgage. The generally accepted view is that the mortgage is still enforceable and may be foreclosed if the obligation is not paid. The running of the statute of limitations renders the obligation unenforceable, but does not discharge it. Because the obligation continues to exist, so does its security. A second view is that the remedy on the mortgage is barred with the remedy on the obligation because the mortgage is dependent on the obligation for its existence and thus, also for its enforceability.

CHAPTER 5

MORTGAGED PROPERTY

I. MORTGAGEABLE INTERESTS

A. GENERAL

Any transferable interest in realty may be mortgaged. Thus, a fee simple, a leasehold, a life estate, a reversion, and a remainder are all mortgageable interests. Although a fee simple is the subject of most mortgages, the leasehold mortgage has become a common financing vehicle. *See* Ch. 3, pp. 69–71 (analyzing leasehold mortgage). The discussion in this book presumes a fee mortgage unless otherwise indicated.

B. MORTGAGING SEPARATE INTERESTS IN SAME LAND

Two or more interests in the same parcel of real estate may be mortgaged independently.

Illustration: L leases a farm to T for a twenty-year term. L mortgages the reversion in fee to A Bank. T mortgages the leasehold to B Bank. Each mortgage is a valid lien on a separate interest in the farm.

C. DESCRIPTION

The mortgagee usually does not take possession of the mortgaged property, at least not before default. *See* Ch. 8, pp. 169–174 (discussing significance of mortgage theories and mortgagee in possession). Thus, the mortgagee generally may impart notice of its lien only by recording the mortgage. It is, therefore, imperative that the mortgaged realty be described accurately in the mortgage. *See* Ch. 9, pp. 186–187 (treating recording statutes).

II. EXTENT OF MORTGAGE COVERAGE

The mortgage lien may attach to certain property not specifically described in the mortgage.

A. AFTER–ACQUIRED PROPERTY

The mortgagee may seek to extend the mortgage lien to land the mortgagor subsequently obtains. The mortgagee usually may achieve this result by inserting an after-acquired property clause in the mortgage. As a general rule, the clause creates an equitable lien on all real estate the mortgagor acquires after the execution of the mortgage.

Illustration: MR owns Blackacre. MR borrows funds from ME. MR executes a note and a mortgage on Blackacre to ME. The mortgage contains an after-acquired property clause. MR purchases Whiteacre. An equitable lien in favor of ME generally attaches to Whiteacre upon its acquisition by MR.

The predominant theory underlying the enforcement of after-acquired property clauses is that the mortgagee is entitled to specific performance of the parties' contractual arrangement. Some states, however, apparently restrict the application of after-acquired property clauses to property functionally related to that initially encumbered.

After-acquired property clauses may be included in corporate mortgages in an attempt to make all of the company's ever-changing real and personal property collateral for the loan. Subject to certain qualifications, personal property as well as realty is covered by an after-acquired property clause. However, the coverage of personalty under such a clause, and related personal property issues, are beyond the scope of this work.

A mortgage containing an after-acquired property clause is outside the chain of title of real estate subsequently obtained by the mortgagor. Hence, purchasers or lienors of such realty from the mortgagor generally will not be on record notice of the mortgagee's equitable lien. The mortgagee, therefore, must take further action to preserve the priority of its lien. It may by mortgage provision require the mortgagor to execute recordable mortgage amendments specifically describing after-acquired land as it is obtained.

B. EASEMENTS

Easements appurtenant to the mortgaged land are part of the property. Thus, they are automatically subject to the mortgage lien irrespective of whether they arise before or after the execution of the mortgage.

C. FIXTURES

A fixture is an item of tangible personal property that becomes realty by virtue of its attachment to land with the intent it remain permanently affixed. The fixture concept presents two real estate finance problems.

The first issue is whether the item in controversy is a fixture. If it is a fixture, the item constitutes part of the mortgaged land and is subject to the mortgage lien without additional description, regardless of whether it became part of the realty before or after the execution of the mortgage. If the item is not a fixture, it is not part of the mortgaged land and hence, is not subject to the mortgage lien unless specifically covered in the mortgage. Most mortgage transactions involve no controversy with respect to identifying fixtures. For example, the parties generally agree that a building on the property is covered by the mortgage. Moveable articles, however, present troublesome questions that should be resolved by the parties at the time the mortgage is negotiated.

Even if the item in question is found to be a fixture subject to the mortgage, a second problem arises. The mortgagee must insure that the mortgage constitutes a first lien on the fixture. This issue is treated in the portion of these materials dealing with lien priorities. *See* Ch. 9, pp. 195–196 (discussing liens on fixtures).

D. CONDEMNATION AWARDS

If all or part of the mortgaged property is taken by eminent domain, the mortgagee's lien attaches to the condemnation award on the theory that the award is a substitute for the realty. When all the mortgaged property is taken, the mortgagee is immediately entitled to satisfy the underlying obligation out of the award. When only part of the mortgaged property is taken, authorities differ regarding how much of the award the mortgagee should receive. Thus, the issue of condemnation is often the subject of extensive negotiation and mortgage provision.

E. INSURANCE PROCEEDS

A casualty insurance policy is a personal indemnification contract. Insurance proceeds generally are not considered to be a substitute for the destroyed property. The mortgagee, therefore, has no interest in the proceeds of a policy obtained by the mortgagor unless the policy specifically insures the interests of both parties.

Mortgages commonly provide that the mortgagor must insure the mortgaged property for the benefit of both the mortgagor and the mortgagee. The mortgagee's interest may be covered by the addition of a clause to the mortgagor's policy. Two types of clauses are used to accomplish this result—the standard mortgage clause and the loss payable or open mortgage clause. The standard mortgagee clause is preferred by lenders because the mortgagee thereby receives an independent right of recovery against the insurer. This right continues even if the mortgagor voids the mortgagor's coverage by violating the terms of the policy. On the other hand, the mortgagee's rights under a loss payable clause are derived from the mortgagor and are lost if the mortgagor negates the mortgagor's coverage by breaching the policy.

When the parties are both insured as required by the mortgage and loss occurs, controversy may arise regarding whether the insurance proceeds should be applied to reconstruction of the premises or to payment of the mortgage debt. When the mortgage is silent on this issue, the generally accepted view is that the mortgagee may choose between these alternatives. There is, however, some authority to the contrary, which holds that under certain circumstances insurance proceeds must be used to rebuild. *See* Starkman v. Sigmond, 446 A.2d 1249 (N.J.Super.Ch.1982).

The application of insurance proceeds often is specifically covered in the mortgage. Sometimes the mortgage provides for rebuilding if certain conditions are met. On other occasions, the mortgage gives the mortgagee the option to use the proceeds for rebuilding or for payment of the debt. Courts generally enforce these clauses as written. However, one court refused to recognize a lender's right to apply proceeds to the debt under an "option" clause where the security was not impaired and the loan payments were current. It found that "good faith" and "fair dealing" required use of the funds for reconstruction. Schoolcraft v. Ross, 146 Cal.Rptr. 57 (Cal.App.1978).

F.   RENTS AND PROFITS

The mortgagee may have the right to receive rents and profits produced by the mortgaged land and apply them to the mortgage debt. *See* Ch. 8, pp. 169–179 (discussing right to possession and rents).

III.   WASTE OF MORTGAGED PROPERTY

A.   DOCTRINE OF WASTE

Once the mortgagee has accepted the real estate as adequate security for the debt, it is concerned, of course, that the mortgagor maintains the mortgaged premises so that the property does not decrease in value. The mortgagor's duties in this regard are generally governed by the doctrine of waste, the principle that prohibits a lawful possessor from physically damaging or destroying the property occupied.

B. MORTGAGEE'S REMEDIES FOR WASTE

When the mortgagor commits waste, the mortgagee generally may pursue one or more of the following courses of action: seek damages, request an injunction, commence foreclosure proceedings.

1. Damages

In title theory states, the mortgagor is treated as a tenant liable for common law waste and the mortgagee is viewed as fictional legal titleholder who can recover actual damages to the realty either before or at foreclosure. In lien theory states, the mortgagor, as owner of the mortgaged property, cannot commit common law waste. That doctrine applies only to acts committed by rightful possessors such as life tenants, lessees, and concurrent owners. Although in lien theory jurisdictions the mortgagee may not recover damages to the real estate, it may recover damages for the impairment of its security interest. Authorities, however, differ as to what constitutes impairment and whether an action for damages may be brought before foreclosure.

2. Injunction

In all jurisdictions, a mortgagee may obtain an injunction against waste when the mortgagor causes the mortgaged realty to diminish in value to the extent that the mortgagee's security is impaired. It is generally agreed that impairment in this case occurs when the property depreciates in value to a point at which the margin between the value of the real estate and the amount of the mortgage debt is less than prudent lenders normally require.

> *Illustration*: MR owns land worth $11,000. MR mortgages the property to ME to secure an $8,000 promissory note. MR cuts timber on the land that reduces it in value to $10,000. Assuming that mortgage lenders generally will not make loans in excess of 80% of the value of the mortgaged property, ME may enjoin MR from cutting more timber.

3. Foreclosure

Mortgages commonly provide that waste is an event of default and therefore, a basis for acceleration and foreclosure.

CHAPTER 6

TRANSFER OF MORTGAGOR'S INTEREST

I. MORTGAGOR'S INTEREST

The precise nature of the mortgagor's interest in the mortgaged property varies among the states depending upon the prevailing mortgage theory. *See* Ch. 1, pp. 8–10 (discussing mortgage theories). Nonetheless, the mortgagor is viewed everywhere as owner of the property for transfer purposes. This is true even in title theory states where the mortgagee holds legal "title" solely as security. *See* Ch. 1, p. 9 (analyzing title theory). As owner of the mortgaged premises, the mortgagor may transfer the property by deed or by will or further encumber it by mortgage. Moreover, the mortgaged property may be transferred by forced sale or by intestate succession. This chapter deals primarily with issues that arise when the mortgagor transfers the mortgaged property by deed.

II. CONVEYANCE OF MORTGAGED PROPERTY

A. MORTGAGOR'S POWER TO CONVEY

The mortgagor may freely convey the mortgaged property. A mortgage provision purporting to prevent conveyance is void as an illegal disabling restraint on alienation. However, as discussed later in this chapter, the mortgage may authorize the mortgagee to accelerate the debt if the mortgagor conveys the mortgaged property without the mortgagee's consent. *See* pp. 123–130 (considering due-on-sale clause).

B.   EFFECT OF CONVEYANCE ON MORTGAGE

When the mortgagor conveys the mortgaged property, it is important to determine whether the mortgage is discharged before title passes or survives the conveyance. The answer depends upon the contractual arrangement between the mortgagor–grantor and the grantee.

1.   Mortgage Is Discharged

The parties frequently agree that the mortgagor will pay off the mortgage debt at closing and transfer the property free from the mortgage lien. (It is assumed that the mortgage documents permit prepayment. *See* Ch. 4, pp. 99–100 (discussing prepayment).) In such case, the purchase price is set at an amount sufficient to pay the mortgagor for the mortgagor's equity in the property and also to satisfy the mortgage debt. If the grantee does not have enough money on hand to pay the purchase price, and the grantee usually does not, the grantee must obtain a new mortgage loan to make up the deficit. The existing mortgage then is discharged and replaced by the new mortgage.

Illustration: MR owns a house encumbered by a $30,000 mortgage held by ME. GE agrees to purchase the property for $90,000. GE has $20,000 cash and obtains a $70,000 loan from Bank. GE pays $60,000 to MR for MR's equity and $30,000 to ME to satisfy the mortgage debt. ME releases its mortgage, and MR deeds the property to GE. GE executes a new $70,000 mortgage to Bank.

2. Mortgage Survives

The parties may agree that the existing mortgage will survive the conveyance. In that event, the grantee pays the mortgagor the value of the mortgagor's equity and takes title subject to the mortgage lien. Even absent such an agreement, a properly recorded mortgage will survive unless it is satisfied at or before closing. *See* Ch. 9, pp. 186–187 (analyzing recording statutes).

C.   RIGHTS AND OBLIGATIONS OF PARTIES WHEN MORTGAGE SURVIVES CONVEYANCE

When the mortgage survives the conveyance, the legal relationship among the mortgagee, the mortgagor, and the grantee depends upon whether the grantee assumes personal responsibility for the underlying obligation.

1.   "Subject to" Conveyance

a.   *Grantee's Rights and Obligations*

If the grantee does not assume the mortgage debt, the conveyance is merely "subject to" the mortgage. Upon default, the mortgagee may fore-close and have the encumbered real estate sold, but as a general rule the mortgagee may not proceed against the "subject to" grantee personally.

Illustration: MR conveys mortgaged property to GE by deed that provides that the conveyance is "subject to" a prior recorded mortgage. This means that GE takes the property subject to the mortgage lien, but generally has no personal responsibility to pay the underlying obligation. The term "subject to" is not a promise from GE to pay the mortgage debt.

As indicated in the immediately preceding illustration, the deed from the mortgagor to the "subject to" grantee usually provides that the grantee takes title subject to the mortgage. Although a provision of this type is not necessary for the survival of a properly recorded mortgage, it is utilized by the mortgagor to limit the mortgagor's liability on the deed's covenants of title by excluding the mortgage from their coverage.

Illustration: MR conveys mortgaged property to GE by general warranty deed that does not mention a prior recorded mortgage. GE takes the property subject to the mortgage because GE is on constructive notice of the recorded instrument. GE, however, may have a cause of action against MR for breach of the deed's present covenant against encumbrances.

Although the "subject to" grantee is not personally liable on the mortgage debt, the grantee commonly pays the obligation to avoid losing the property by foreclosure.

b. *Mortgagor's Rights and Obligations*

The mortgagor remains personally liable on the debt following a "subject to" conveyance unless released by the mortgagee. When not released, the mortgagor becomes a surety, liable to the extent the land proves to be of insufficient value to satisfy the debt. As a surety, the mortgagor generally is still subject to suit by the mortgagee directly on the underlying obligation and is liable for any deficiency resulting from a foreclosure sale. *See* Ch. 8, pp. 184–185 (discussing recovery on note alone/"one action" rule). If, however, the mortgagor is forced to pay the entire debt, the mortgagor typically is subrogated to the mortgagee's rights and can foreclose in order to be reimbursed to the extent of the value of the land.

Illustration: MR executes a $10,000 promissory note and a mortgage to ME. MR then conveys the mortgaged property to GE by deed which provides that title is "subject to" the mortgage. The parties make no agreement regarding payment of the note. GE fails to pay the note. ME generally may either (1) foreclose and seek a deficiency judgment against MR if the sale proceeds are insufficient to satisfy the debt or (2) bring suit against MR on the note without foreclosing. ME chooses the second alternative, which is normally available. MR pays ME $10,000 and is subrogated to ME's right to foreclose. MR forecloses; the property brings $8,000 at sale. MR is entitled to the $8,000, but MR ordinarily must absorb a $2,000 loss because GE had no personal liability on the note.

2. "Assumption" Conveyance

a. *Grantee's Rights and Obligations*

A grantee taking land encumbered by a mortgage may personally assume liability for the mortgage debt. When that occurs, the transaction is termed an "assumption" conveyance. Although the assumption may be accomplished outside the conveyance, it is usually based on a clause in the deed to the effect that the grantee "assumes and agrees to pay" the mortgage debt. When the grantee accepts a deed containing a clause of this type, the grantee also accepts personal responsibility for the debt.

The mortgagor, as one of the contracting parties, of course may enforce the assumption contract. The mortgagee also may enforce the contract against the grantee under either of two theories. (1) The generally accepted view is that the mortgagee is a third party beneficiary of the assumption contract. (2) Some courts consider the mortgagee's rights against the grantee as "derived" under equitable principles from the mortgagor's rights in the assumption contract. In either case, the consequence of an "assumption" conveyance is that, upon default, the mortgagee may foreclose and also obtain a deficiency judgment against the grantee. Furthermore, in most jurisdictions the mortgagee may obtain judgment against the grantee on the obligation without foreclosing the mortgage. Some derivative theory states, however, refuse the mortgagee this right on the ground that the grantee is not liable on the assumption contract until the mortgagor suffers actual loss. *See also* Ch. 8, pp. 184–185 (discussing "one action" rule).

b. *Mortgagor's Rights and Obligations*

The grantee's assumption of personal responsibility for the mortgage debt does not relieve the mortgagor of liability. *But see* p. 130 (considering federal regulation that apparently requires the mortgagee to release the mortgagor in certain situations). Again the mortgagor becomes a surety, this time liable for any deficiency resulting from a foreclosure sale and in most jurisdictions, subject to direct suit on the debt. *But see* Ch. 8, pp. 184–185 (analyzing "one action" rule). The mortgagor is, however, in a much better position in an "assumption" conveyance than in a "subject to" transfer. First, because the assuming grantee is personally liable on the underlying obligation, the grantee has greater incentive to pay than when the grantee only risks loss of the land on default. Second, if the mortgagor pays the debt, the mortgagor is subrogated to the mortgagee's rights and may look to both the land and the grantee personally for reimbursement. Third, it is commonly recognized that the mortgagor may sue the defaulting grantee for breach of the assumption contract without first having paid the mortgage debt and apply monies recovered toward satisfaction of the debt.

   Illustration: MR executes a $30,000 promissory note and a mortgage to ME. MR then conveys the mortgaged property to GE by deed that provides that GE assumes and agrees to pay the mortgage debt. GE fails to pay. In most states, ME may either (1) foreclose and seek a deficiency judgment against MR and GE if the sale proceeds are insufficient to satisfy the note, (2) bring suit against MR on the note without foreclosing, or (3) bring suit against GE on the note without foreclosing. ME chooses the second alternative, which is widely available. MR pays ME $30,000 and is subrogated to ME's rights against GE. MR may now either (1) foreclose and recover any deficiency from GE or (2) sue GE directly on the note and the assumption contract without foreclosing.

c.   *Successive "Assumption" Conveyances/Break in Chain of Assumptions*

When successive "assumption" conveyances are made, each grantee is personally liable on the mortgage debt. The last assuming grantee, however, bears primary responsibility.

   Illustration: MR executes a $20,000 note and a mortgage to ME. MR makes an "assumption" conveyance to GE–1 who in turn makes an "assumption" conveyance to GE–2 who defaults. ME forecloses and receives $18,000 from the foreclosure sale. ME obtains a $2,000 deficiency judgment against GE–1. If GE–1 pays, GE–1 has the right to obtain reimbursement from GE–2.

If the chain of assumptions is broken by a "subject to" conveyance, authorities are divided on whether grantees who assume after the break are personally liable on the mortgage debt. In jurisdictions that view the mortgagee as a third party beneficiary of the assumption contract, a subsequent assuming grantee generally is liable. Some courts, however, have found the grantee free from liability on the ground that the parties did not intend the mortgagee to benefit from the assumption. In derivative theory states, a grantee who assumes after a break is not liable because the mortgagee has no claim against the "subject to" grantee and therefore, cannot derive rights from that individual's assumption contract with a subsequent grantee.

d.   Termination or Modification of Assumption Contract

Authorities also disagree as to whether the mortgagee's rights against an assuming grantee are affected when the grantee is released from the assumption contract by the grantor. In most third party beneficiary theory states, the mortgagee's rights survive the release if the mortgagee accepted or relied on the assumption agreement prior to the release. In a few third party beneficiary jurisdictions, the mortgagee's rights survive the release in all cases on the theory that the mortgagee's rights vested immediately upon the execution of the assumption contract. In derivative theory states, the mortgagee's rights are destroyed by the release unless the mortgagee has previously filed a foreclosure suit or it would be inequitable to enforce the release.

A similar diversity of opinion exists on the question of whether the mortgagee's rights are affected by modification of the assumption contract.

3. Extension Problem

The grantee normally pays the mortgage debt in both the "subject to" and the "assumption" conveyance situations. If the grantee has difficulty doing so, the mortgagee may extend the time for payment. Serious collateral consequences may result. The extension may operate to discharge the mortgagor in whole or in part on the theory that it impairs the mortgagor's right as a surety to pay the debt at maturity and to be subrogated to the mortgagee's position at that time.

An extension granted an assuming grantee typically operates to completely discharge the mortgagor. This is because the extension denies the mortgagor subrogation rights against the grantee for the entire debt. The rule, however, operates to discharge the mortgagor only if the mortgagee had knowledge of the assumption when it granted the extension.

Authorities differ as to the effect of an extension granted a "subject to" grantee. The generally accepted view is that the mortgagor is discharged to the extent of the value of the land at the time the extension was granted. This is because the extension costs the mortgagor the opportunity to be subrogated to the mortgagee's right to foreclose. Some states go further and completely discharge the mortgagor in this situation. Other jurisdictions consider the mortgagor's liability to be unaffected by the extension.

These rules on discharge are subject to two important qualifications. First, the mortgagor is discharged only by an extension agreement that is legally binding on the mortgagee. Mere inaction by the mortgagee after default does not constitute such an extension. Second, even when the grantee obtains a binding extension, the mortgagor is not discharged if the mortgagor consents to the arrangement. Consequently, mortgages commonly provide that the mortgagee may grant extensions to subsequent grantees without affecting the mortgagor's liability.

D.   ACQUISITION BY MORTGAGEE

A mortgagee may acquire the mortgaged realty from the mortgagor by a transaction separate and distinct from the mortgage agreement. Acquisitions of this type do not violate the rule that prohibits contemporaneous clogs of the mortgagor's equity of redemption. *See* Ch. 1, p. 5 (discussing clogging). Such transactions, however, are subject to strict judicial scrutiny so that the mortgagor is protected from the ordinarily superior bargaining power of the mortgagee. If the acquisition is made in bad faith or for inadequate consideration, courts will not recognize it, and the mortgagor will continue to hold an equity of redemption.

1. Deed in Lieu of Foreclosure

Mortgagees often acquire mortgaged property by deed in lieu of foreclosure. Upon default, the mortgagee typically is willing to cancel the mortgage debt and accept a deed to the mortgaged property in lieu of foreclosing the mortgagor's equity of redemption. Such transactions generally are advantageous to both parties. The mortgagee bypasses the frequently complex, expensive, and protracted foreclosure process. The mortgagor sidesteps a potential deficiency judgment. Moreover, each avoids the public attention engendered by foreclosure. *See* Ch. 8, pp. 182–185 (discussing alternatives to foreclosure).

2. Merger

The doctrine of merger provides that when successive real property interests come into the same hands, the lesser interest ends by merging into the greater interest. Thus, when the mortgagee acquires the mortgaged real estate, the mortgage normally merges into the fee. However, because merger is predicated on the actual or presumed intention of the owner of both interests, the mortgage generally is preserved if merger would be detrimental to the mortgagee.

Illustration: MR owns Blackacre subject to a first mortgage to ME–1 and a second mortgage to

ME–2. MR conveys Blackacre to ME–1. Merger does not occur unless ME–1, with knowledge of the mortgage held by ME–2, expresses the intent for it to do so. It is presumed that ME–1 does not intend to gratuitously benefit ME–2 by giving ME–2's mortgage first lien priority.

III. DUE–ON–SALE CLAUSE

A. GENERAL

Although the mortgagee cannot prohibit the mortgagor from transferring the mortgaged property, the mortgagee may include a provision in the mortgage giving it the right to accelerate the debt if the mortgaged property is conveyed without its consent. A mortgage provision of this type is known as a due-on-sale clause. Such clauses are often broadly worded to cover the transfer of any interest in the property. Transfer by land contract, lease, or junior encumbrance, as well as by outright conveyance, are therefore acts that may trigger acceleration of the debt.

Mortgagees today may freely enforce due-on-sale clauses upon most transfers of mortgaged real estate. A federal statute, discussed later in this section, so mandates. The current situation, however, is a product of years of litigation, regulation, and legislation on the subject. This historical background is traced below.

B. STATE LAW BACKGROUND

At one time, considerable controversy existed regarding the enforceability of due-on-sale clauses. At the beginning of the 1980s, the states were divided into two camps: those following the "automatic enforcement" approach and those subscribing to the "impairment of security" view. This split of authority was primarily the result of differing judicial attitudes as to whether the enforcement of a due-on-sale clause constituted an unreasonable restraint on alienation.

1. Automatic Enforcement Approach

Courts adopting the automatic enforcement approach generally reasoned as follows: To the extent enforcement of a due-on-sale clause directly or indirectly limits the mortgagor's ability to convey the mortgaged realty, such restraint on alienation is reasonable. Mortgagees are justified in using a contractual provision to get rid of low-interest-rate loans in order to maintain their lending portfolios at or near the current market interest rate. Moreover, mortgagors in general benefit from a rule permitting mortgagees to enforce due-on-sale clauses at their discretion. The acceleration of low-interest-rate loans creates additional funds for new borrowers. It also tends to reduce the overall mortgage interest rate by alleviating the mortgagees' need to charge exceptionally high rates on new mortgage loans in order to compensate for low returns on outstanding loans.

Some state courts that adopted the automatic enforcement approach used markedly different analysis in doing so. They determined that due-on-sale clauses are not restraints on alienation in any sense and therefore, are enforceable contract provisions. *See, e.g.*, Occidental Savings and Loan Association v. Venco Partnership, 293 N.W.2d 843 (Neb. 1980).

2. Impairment of Security View

Courts in a number of states found due-on-sale clauses enforceable only if the mortgagee established that the conveyance in question would impair the security or enhance the likelihood of default. These courts concluded that it is unreasonable for a mortgagee to exercise a due-on-sale clause merely to improve its financial condition. Additional justification is necessary to tip the balance to the reasonable side of the scale. The grantee's present financial situation, credit history, and background respecting property use and maintenance are factors relevant to this determination.

Some courts espousing the impairment of security point of view concluded that automatic enforcement of a due-on-sale clause constitutes an unreasonable restraint on alienation. *See, e.g.*, Wellenkamp v. Bank of America, 148 Cal.Rptr. 379 (Cal.1978). Other courts adopted the impairment of security view on another theory. They reasoned that it is inequitable for a mortgagee to accelerate the debt under a due-on-sale clause solely for economic reasons. The results of this approach were essentially the same as produced by the restraint on alienation analysis. In addition, some state legislatures enacted statutes incorporating the impairment of security approach.

3. Resolution

As state law became increasingly fractured along the lines discussed above, pressure mounted for a resolution for the due-on-sale clause conflict. The federal government became involved, and in the end, Congress settled the matter by statute. Following is an overview of significant federal activity in the due-on-sale clause area.

C. FEDERAL HOME LOAN BANK BOARD REGULATIONS

The Federal Home Loan Bank Board (today the Office of Thrift Supervision) in 1976 authorized federal savings and loan associations to freely enforce due-on-sale clauses upon most transfers of mortgaged real estate. 12 C.F.R. § 545.8–3(f) & (g) (1982). There was some question, however, as to whether this regulation preempted restrictive state laws on the subject. The Supreme Court answered the preemption question in the affirmative in Fidelity Federal Savings and Loan Association v. de la Cuesta, 458 U.S. 141 (1982), thereby eliminating any doubt about the authority of federal savings and loan associations in this area.

D. GARN—ST. GERMAIN DEPOSITORY INSTITUTIONS ACT OF 1982

1. General

Because of the fragmented law on the enforceability of due-on-sale clauses and the adverse economic impact of due-on-sale restrictions on lending institutions, Congress included provisions in the Garn—St. Germain Depository Institutions Act of 1982 preempting state due-on-sale law and establishing a national standard for the enforcement of due-on-sale clauses. 12 U.S.C.A. § 1701j–3. As a general proposition, the Act permits mortgagees to freely enforce due-on-sale clauses. There are, however, exceptions to this basic rule—one for "window period" loans that is largely only of historical interest and another for certain transfers of residential mortgaged property that retains its vitality.

2. Window Period Loan Exception

A window period loan is one made or assumed before the effective date of the Act (October 15, 1982) in a jurisdiction that had a statewide restriction on the enforcement of due-on-sale clauses in place at the time the loan was executed or assumed. Window period loans remained subject to the restrictive state law for three years (until October 15, 1985) unless the appropriate regulatory body for the originating lender provided otherwise. 12 U.S.C.A. § 1701j–3(c). Under this scheme, state legislatures were given the power to "otherwise regulate" window period loans made by lenders that are not federally chartered. Lawmakers in a few window period jurisdictions extended state law restrictions on such window period loans for various periods beyond October 15, 1985.

Mortgage loans made by federal savings and loan associations were specifically excluded from the window period exception. This is, of course, consistent with the *de la Cuesta* decision discussed above.

3. Exempt Transfers

The Act permanently exempts certain transfers of residential mortgaged property "containing less than five dwelling units." Mortgagees are prohibited from enforcing a due-on-sale clause in the following residential transfer situations: "(1) the creation of a lien or other encumbrance subordinate to the lender's security instrument which does not relate to a transfer of rights of occupancy in the property; (2) the creation of a purchase money security interest for household appliances; (3) a transfer by devise, descent, or operation of law on the death of a joint tenant or tenant by the entirety; (4) the granting of a leasehold interest of three years or less not containing an option to purchase; (5) a transfer to a relative resulting from the death of a borrower; (6) a transfer where the spouse or children of the borrower become an owner of the property; (7) a transfer resulting from a decree of a dissolution of marriage, legal separation agreement, or from an incidental property settlement agreement, by which the spouse of the borrower becomes an owner of the property; (8) a transfer into an inter vivos trust in which the borrower is and remains a beneficiary and which does not relate to a transfer of rights of occupancy in the property; or (9) any other transfer or disposition described in regulations prescribed by the Federal Home Loan Bank Board." 12 U.S.C.A. § 1701j–3(d).

4. Role of Office of Thrift Supervision

A final note of caution is in order. The Office of Thrift Supervision (OTS) (formerly the Federal Home Loan Bank Board) is empowered to promulgate rules, regulations, and interpretations of the Act that apply to all lenders. 12 U.S.C.A. § 1701j–3(e)(1). OTS activity in this area should be consulted because the Act raises, but does not answer, numerous practical questions. *See* 12 C.F.R. §§ 591.1–591.6 (2008) for OTS regulations.

E. PRACTICAL CONSIDERATIONS

When the mortgage contains an enforceable due-on-sale clause and the mortgagor desires to transfer the mortgaged property, the mortgagee has several alternatives, which include the following:

(1) The mortgagee may withhold consent to the transfer, accelerate the debt upon transfer, and then reinvest the funds at the current market interest rate. Some lenders also have sought a prepayment penalty under these circumstances, but such attempts generally have been rejected by the courts on the ground that once the lender accelerates the debt there can no longer be any *pre*payment. Moreover, Office of Thrift Supervision regulations issued

under the Garn—St. Germain Depository Institutions Act of 1982 prohibit mortgagees from charging a prepayment penalty in connection with the enforcement of a due-on-sale clause in a mortgage on a borrower-occupied residence. 12 C.F.R. § 591.5(b)(2) (2008). *See* Ch. 4, pp. 99–100 (discussing prepayment penalties).

(2) The mortgagee may consent to the transfer conditioned upon the grantee's assumption of the mortgage and the payment of a transfer fee or an increased interest rate. The Garn—St. Germain Depository Institutions Act of 1982 contains an unusual provision that "encourage[s]" the lender to consent to transfer upon the grantee's assumption of the mortgage at a blended interest rate not more than the average of the original rate and the current market rate. 12 U.S.C.A. § 1701j–3(b)(3). If the lender consents to an assumption of a loan on a borrower-occupied residence, it apparently must by regulation release the mortgagor from personal liability. 12 C.F.R. § 591.5(b)(4) (2008). This regulation, however, has been interpreted in various ways.

(3) The mortgagee may promote customer relations by consenting to the transfer without imposing any conditions.

IV. FURTHER ENCUMBRANCE OF MORTGAGED PROPERTY

A mortgagor may place a junior mortgage on the mortgaged property. *See* Ch. 2, pp. 29–30 (discussing creation of junior mortgages). Such further encumbrance, however, may permit the mortgagee to accelerate the debt under a due-on-sale clause, at least when the mortgaged property is commercial or multi-unit residential in excess of four units. *See* p. 123 (analyzing coverage of due-on-sale clause); pp. 128–129 (listing transfers exempt from operation of due-on-sale clause).

V. TRANSFER AT MORTGAGOR'S DEATH

On the mortgagor's death, the mortgaged property passes to the mortgagor's heirs or devisees. Because the mortgage debt is a personal obligation, the heir or devisee generally may compel the decedent's personal representative to pay the debt. In some states, however, statutes relieve the personal estate of this burden. In addition, specific testamentary directions regarding the payment of mortgage debts may render the general rule inapplicable in individual cases.

CHAPTER 7

TRANSFER OF MORTGAGEE'S INTEREST

I. MORTGAGEE'S INTEREST

Legal problems that arise from the transfer of the mortgagee's interest are some of the most complicated in real estate finance. This is primarily because the mortgagee's interest in the mortgage loan consists of two types of property—the obligation which is personalty and the mortgage which is realty. The material in this chapter is more easily understood if the reader remains constantly aware of this duality.

II. ASSIGNMENT OF MORTGAGE LOAN

A. BASIC CONCEPT

A mortgage cannot be transferred except in connection with the transfer of the obligation it secures. *See* Ch. 1, p. 2 (discussing obligation/security distinction). This principle has two facets. First, when the mortgagee assigns only the underlying debt, the mortgage is automatically carried to the assignee as an inseparable incident of the debt. The assignee then may require the mortgagee to execute a formal mortgage assignment. Second, when the mortgagee assigns only the mortgage, the transaction generally is invalid, and the assignee acquires no interest in either the mortgage or the debt. If, however, the mortgagee intends the separate mortgage assignment to operate also as an assignment of the secured indebtedness, the transaction usually is valid, and the assignee receives an equitable right to the debt.

Illustration: MR executes a promissory note and a mortgage to ME. ME assigns the note to A who purchases it without knowledge that it is secured by the mortgage. Nonetheless, A has an equitable right to the mortgage. ME holds the mortgage in trust for A and must transfer it to A upon request.

Illustration: MR executes a promissory note and a mortgage to ME. ME assigns the mortgage to A, but keeps the note under the mistaken belief that both parties (ME and A) have rights against MR. The attempted transfer is ineffective. A acquires no interest in the mortgage loan.

Illustration: MR executes a promissory note and a mortgage to ME. ME gives the note to ME's attorney X for safekeeping. Later ME requests X to return the note so that ME can transfer it to A. X refuses on the ground that ME has failed to pay for legal services rendered. Undeterred, ME assigns the mortgage to A with the express intention that the assignment also operate as an assignment of the note. The assignment is effective.

A may enforce both the note and mortgage subject to X's lien rights, if any. See Beaty v. Inlet Beach, Inc., 9 So.2d 735 (Fla.1942). (As a general rule, an assignee must gain possession of a negotiable note in order to enforce it. *See* UCC §§ 3–203, 3–301.)

The usual transfer of a mortgage loan involves separate assignments of the obligation and the mortgage. The validity of the assignment of the underlying obligation is determined by reference to contract and commercial paper law. The formal assignment of the mortgage must comply with the legal requirements for the conveyance of an interest in land.

B.   ORDINARY ASSIGNMENT/ ASSIGNMENT AS SECURITY DISTINCTION

An ordinary assignment of a note and mortgage must be distinguished from an assignment of a note and mortgage as security (collateral assignment). An ordinary assignment involves the sale of a note and mortgage to an assignee (purchaser). A collateral assignment involves the pledge of a note and mortgage to secure a loan from a collateral assignee (lender). The bulk of this chapter focuses on the ordinary sale assignment and the legal status of the assignee. One section deals exclusively with collateral assignments. *See* pp. 160–161 (assignment as security).

C.   ASSIGNEE'S RIGHTS

The assignee of a properly transferred note and mortgage is entitled to collect payment of the debt from the mortgagor and in the event of default, is empowered to foreclose the mortgage. The assignee's rights, however, are subject to the limitations discussed in the following sections on defenses that may be available against the assignee and on payment problems that may arise after the assignment.

D.   APPLICABILITY OF UCC ARTICLE 9

Article 9 of the Uniform Commercial Code (UCC) now covers ordinary assignments (sales) of mortgage loans in addition to assignments of mortgage loans as security. *See* UCC § 9–109(a) & (b). *See also* pp. 160–161 (discussing assignments as security). Under Article 9, an assignee (purchaser) of a promissory note and mortgage is shielded from claims of the mortgagee-assignor's future lien creditors and bankruptcy trustee without recording in the real estate records, filing under the UCC, possessing the note, or doing anything else. In other words, the assignment (sale) is "perfected" automatically. *See* UCC § 9–309(4). *See also* pp. 147–150 (considering conflicting assignments).

E.   RECORDING MORTGAGE ASSIGNMENT

The assignee must record the mortgage assignment to preserve its interest against subsequent purchasers or encumbrancers of the mortgaged property in the event the mortgagee-assignor improperly releases the mortgage. *See* Ch. 9, pp. 186–187 (discussing recording statutes).

Illustration: MR owns land worth $20,000. MR executes a $10,000 promissory note and a mortgage on the property to ME. ME assigns and delivers the documents to A, but A does not record. ME and MR enter into a scheme to defraud A. ME executes a release of the mortgage to MR who records it. MR then conveys the land to Y, an innocent purchaser, for $20,000, an amount that is twice as much as MR normally could have obtained. *See* Ch. 6, pp. 112–113 (analyzing effect of conveyance on mortgage). Y owns the land free from the mortgage because the land records did not reflect A's current lien on the property. A's only recourse is against MR and ME.

Recording also may protect the assignee if the mortgagee-assignor should assign the same note and mortgage to another party, at least under the traditional approach. *See* pp. 147–150 (analyzing conflicting assignments). Moreover, in some circumstances recording imparts notice that mortgage loan payments should be directed to the assignee. *See* pp. 141–147 (discussing payment problems after assignment).

In response to problems associated with recording numerous and frequent mortgage assignments, entities connected with the secondary mortgage market devised the Mortgage Electronic Registration

System (MERS). Under this privately organized, funded, and managed scheme, MERS becomes the nominal record holder of entered mortgages and then maintains current information on-line about assignments and other aspects of these mortgage loans.

F.   SECONDARY MORTGAGE MARKET

The assignment process occurs innumerable times each business day. Many mortgagees originate mortgage loans and then sell and assign them to permanent investors. The aggregate of these assignment transactions constitutes the secondary mortgage market. *See* Ch. 2, pp. 37–39 (describing secondary mortgage market support institutions); Ch. 2, pp. 27–28 (discussing mortgaged-backed securities).

III.   DEFENSES AVAILABLE AGAINST ASSIGNEE

As a general rule, the right of an assignee of a mortgage loan to foreclosure the mortgage upon default depends on its ability to enforce the underlying obligation. This doctrine rests on the basic concept that the obligation is the essential aspect of the transaction, while the mortgage is just an appendage. The form of the underlying obligation (negotiable/nonnegotiable), therefore, is of primary importance in determining what defenses the mortgagor may assert against an assignee of the mortgage loan.

A. NONNEGOTIABLE OBLIGATION

If the underlying obligation is nonnegotiable, the assignee takes the note and the mortgage subject to all defenses the mortgagor had against the mortgagee.

> *Illustration*: ME agrees to loan $3,000 to MR. MR executes a $3,000 nonnegotiable note and a mortgage to ME. ME, however, does not actually advance any money to MR. ME immediately assigns the documents to A, who is a bona fide purchaser for value without notice of ME's failure to advance funds. MR refuses to pay A. A cannot recover on the note nor can A foreclose the mortgage; A took the documents subject to MR's defense of failure of consideration.

B. NEGOTIABLE OBLIGATION

It is more difficult to determine what defenses the mortgagor may assert against an assignee when the underlying obligation is negotiable. The answer primarily depends upon whether the assignee qualifies as a holder in due course. An assignee may become a holder in due course only if certain requirements are met. First, the obligation, of course, must be negotiable. *See* UCC § 3–104(a). Second, it must have been transferred to the assignee by negotiation. *See* UCC § 3–201. Third, the assignee must have obtained the obligation for value, in good faith, and without notice of any defect, such as an alteration, claim, or defense. *See* UCC § 3–302(a).

If the underlying obligation is negotiable and the assignee is a holder in due course, the assignee normally takes the note *and* the mortgage free from "personal" defenses the mortgagor had against the mortgagee. *But see* Ch. 2, pp. 50–51 (discussing predatory lending). Personal defenses include mistake, failure of consideration, and fraud in the inducement. *See* UCC § 3–305.

The negotiable mortgage concept rests on the theory that negotiable notes should be freely transferable and that the mortgage, as mere security, should travel with the note. A handful of jurisdictions, however, apparently reject this principle on the ground that a mortgage is a property interest for all purposes and thus, cannot assume the characteristics of commercial paper. Under this minority approach, even a holder in due course takes the mortgage subject to personal defenses the mortgagor had against the mortgagee.

Illustration: ME agrees to loan $3,000 to MR. MR executes a $3,000 negotiable note and a mortgage to ME. However, ME does not actually advance any money to MR. ME immediately negotiates the note and assigns the mortgage to A, a holder in due course. As a holder in due course, A takes the note free from any personal defenses MR had against ME. The defense of failure of consideration is a personal defense. A, therefore, may recover $3,000 on the note from MR. In the vast majority of states, A also may foreclose. This result is based on the theory that the mortgage is clothed with the negotiable characteristics of the note and thus, A also takes the mortgage free from personal defenses. In a handful of jurisdictions, however, A apparently cannot foreclose. This view is predicated on the notion that a mortgage can never become negotiable and therefore, MR can assert MR's personal defense in a foreclosure suit.

Even if the assignee qualifies as a holder in due course, it still takes subject to "real" defenses the mortgagor has on the negotiable obligation. Real defenses include incapacity, duress, infancy, and fraud in the fact. *See* UCC § 3–305(a)(1) & (b).

> *Illustration*: Assume the same fact situation as in the immediately preceding illustration except that MR was mentally incompetent at the time MR executed the note and mortgage. Even though the note is negotiable and A is a holder in due course, A takes the note subject to the real defense of incapacity. Because MR has a valid defense against enforcement of the negotiable note, MR also has a defense against enforcement of the mortgage. Thus, A can neither recover on the note nor foreclose.

Of course, if the assignee does not qualify as a holder in due course, it takes the note and the mortgage subject to both real and personal defenses the mortgagor had against the mortgagee. *See* UCC § 3–305(a).

C. ESTOPPEL CERTIFICATE

A prospective assignee may be unwilling to accept an assignment of a mortgage loan unless it receives an estoppel certificate from the mortgagor specifying the unpaid balance of the obligation and stating that the mortgagor claims no defenses against its enforcement. The assignee may thereby protect itself from all defenses, whether real or personal.

IV. PAYMENT PROBLEMS AFTER ASSIGNMENT

The assignee of a mortgage loan is entitled to receive all payments made after the assignment. Nonetheless, the mortgagor or a grantee may continue to pay the original mortgagee through inadvertence or ignorance. In most instances, the original mortgagee merely forwards the payment to the assignee, and the parties eventually work out the administrative details. Problems arise, however, when the original mortgagee absconds with the funds or becomes insolvent. Who bears the loss, the payor or the assignee? In order to answer this question, one must ascertain who made the payment (the mortgagor or a grantee), the form of obligation involved (negotiable or nonnegotiable), and the type of payment made (part or final). Because the mortgage is a mere incident of the obligation, contract and commercial paper law generally dictates the outcome. The result is not always consistent with the policy underlying the recording statutes.

A. PAYMENT BY MORTGAGOR

1. Negotiable Obligation

a. Established Principles

If the underlying obligation is negotiable, the commonly accepted view is that the mortgagor pays the original mortgagee at the mortgagor's peril. Proper payment, whether part or full, ordinarily can be made only to the holder of a negotiable instrument. *See* UCC § 3–602(a). The mortgagor is protected by the right to demand production of the instrument and its surrender if the payment is final, or an endorsement thereon of part payment if that is the case. If, however, the holder is not a holder in due course and the mortgagor paid the original mortgagee without notice of the prior assignment, the mortgagor may be able to assert successfully the contract defense of payment against the holder. *See* UCC § 3–305(a)(2).

In a handful of states, statutes authorize the mortgagor to pay the mortgagee until an assignment of the mortgage is recorded. Such statutes, of course, run contrary to basic commercial paper policy stated above.

b. Amended UCC Position

UCC § 3–602 was amended to significantly modify the basic pay-the-holder requirement in 2002. The UCC now permits the mortgagor to pay a negotiable obligation to the mortgagee until the mortgagor receives "adequate" notice of a mortgage loan assignment and of the duty to pay the assignee. Such notice must identify the instrument, include a payment address, and bear the signature of the mortgagee or the assignee. *See* UCC § 3–602(b). The pace at which states will enact this amendment is unpredictable.

2.   Nonnegotiable Obligation: Notice Problem

If the underlying obligation is nonnegotiable, the mortgagor may safely pay the mortgagee until receiving notice of an assignment. However, the mortgagor may obtain notice in various ways and frequently is on notice of an assignment.

a.   *Actual Notice*

The mortgagor may receive actual notice of the assignment from the assignor, the assignee, or otherwise.

b.   *Record Notice*

The recordation of a mortgage assignment generally is not considered constructive notice to the mortgagor because recording imparts notice only to subsequent purchasers, not to prior interest holders. There is, however, some authority that recording the assignment puts the mortgagor on notice.

c.   *Inquiry Notice*

By weight of authority, the mortgagor receives inquiry notice of an assignment if upon final payment the mortgagee does not produce and surrender the note or give a reasonable excuse for its inability to do so. This view is based on the belief that it is prudent business practice for the mortgagor to demand production of a nonnegotiable note when paying it off. In some jurisdictions, however, the mortgagor is not on inquiry notice of an assignment when the mortgagee fails to produce the note upon final payment. This stance is supported by the fact that the assignee could have easily protected itself by notifying the mortgagor of the assignment.

The mortgagor's part payment of a nonnegotiable obligation is viewed in a different light. It is not common business practice to require production of a nonnegotiable note upon part payment. The mortgagor, therefore, is typically not on inquiry notice of an assignment just because the mortgagee fails to produce the note each time an installment payment is made.

B. PAYMENT BY GRANTEE

When the mortgagor transfers the mortgaged property to another party, additional payment problems arise.

1. Negotiable Obligation

a. *Established Principles*

If the underlying obligation is negotiable, the grantee ordinarily must pay the holder of the note. *See* UCC § 3–602(a). The grantee cannot safely pay the mortgage owner of record because commercial paper law makes a negotiable instrument freely transferable. The grantee, therefore, must demand production of the note before making either part or full payment. However, the defenses discussed above in connection with payment of a negotiable obligation by the mortgagor also may be available to a grantee.

b. Amended UCC Position

The notice provisions of amended UCC § 3–602, as analyzed in the immediately preceding section on payment by the mortgagee, apply to payment by a grantee as well. *See* UCC § 3–602(b).

2. Nonnegotiable Obligation: Notice Problem

If the underlying obligation is nonnegotiable, the grantee may pay the mortgagee until the grantee receives notice of an assignment. Again notice may come from several sources.

a. Actual Notice

The grantee may receive actual notice of the assignment from the mortgagor, the assignor, the assignee, or otherwise.

b. Record Notice

The grantee also may receive notice from the public records. A properly recorded mortgage assignment is constructive notice to a subsequent grantee.

> *Illustration*: MR executes a nonnegotiable note and a mortgage to ME. ME assigns the documents to A who records the mortgage assignment. MR then sells and conveys the mortgaged proper-

ty to GE subject to the mortgage. GE has no actual knowledge of the assignment, so GE makes part payment to ME. The payment is not good against A. GE was on constructive notice of A's interest because the records reflected the assignment at the time GE purchased the mortgaged property.

c. Inquiry Notice

The grantee generally may receive inquiry notice of an assignment in the same fashion as the mortgagor. Thus the discussion of inquiry notice found in the above section on payment by the mortgagor is applicable here.

C. SERVICING ARRANGEMENTS

The severity of the established general rule that the mortgagor or a grantee ordinarily must pay the holder of a negotiable instrument is softened by the realities of mortgage financing. Often the assignee of the negotiable note and mortgage will authorize the mortgagee to "service" the loan. *See* Ch. 2, pp. 17–18 (analyzing differences among originating/servicing/holding and discussing transfer of servicing rights); Ch. 2, p. 46 (discussing RESPA provisions regarding servicing). The mortgagee thereby continues to collect payments, but now as agent for the assignee. Naturally, such payments are good against the servicing agent's principal—the holder of the negotiable note.

Servicing arrangements also may affect the application of legal principles governing the payment of nonnegotiable obligations. Even if the mortgagor or a grantee has notice of an assignment, payment of a nonnegotiable obligation to the mortgagee will be effective if the mortgagee is servicing the mortgage loan for the assignee. (This analysis applies as well to the payment of assigned negotiable instruments in states that have enacted amended UCC § 3–602 with its notice provision.)

V. CONFLICTING ASSIGNMENTS

An unscrupulous or careless mortgagee may sell and assign the mortgage loan to two or more parties. The conflict among these assignees is not easily resolved. The traditional approach to this issue has two branches—one for nonnegotiable obligations and another for negotiable obligations. Article 9 of the UCC now also addresses the conflicting assignments question, but in a somewhat different manner. Since the traditional approach provides relevant background for the Article 9 approach and to a certain extent coexists with Article 9, both approaches are analyzed in this section.

A.   TRADITIONAL APPROACH

1. Nonnegotiable Obligation

Under the traditional approach, if the underlying obligation is nonnegotiable, priority among assignees is generally governed by applicable real estate recording statutes. This means that the first assignee prevails unless a subsequent assignee fits within

the protection afforded by the local recording statute. *See* Ch. 9, pp. 186–187 (discussing recording
statutes).

   Illustration: MR executes a nonnegotiable note
   and a mortgage to ME. ME sells, assigns, and
   delivers the documents to A–1 who records the
   mortgage assignment. ME then sells and assigns
   to A–2, but, of course, cannot deliver the documents. A–1 and A–2 each claim ownership of the
   mortgage documents. A–1 prevails over A–2, because A–1 recorded first and A–2 received constructive notice of A–1's prior assignment from
   the real estate records. A–2 also received inquiry
   notice from ME's failure to deliver the documents.

2. Negotiable Obligation

   Under the traditional approach, if the underlying
obligation is negotiable, commercial paper law, not
a recording statute, usually determines the rights of
competing assignees. Hence, the assignee who takes
possession of the note and the mortgage normally
prevails.

   Illustration: MR executes a negotiable note and
   a mortgage to ME who records. ME sells and
   assigns the loan to A–1, but retains possession of
   the documents. A–1 records the mortgage assignment. ME then sells the loan to A–2. ME negotiates the note, assigns the mortgage, and delivers
   the documents to A–2 who takes in good faith
   without actual notice of the prior assignment. A–
   1 and A–2 each claim ownership of the note and

the mortgage. Under the commonly accepted view, A–2 prevails over A–1 because constructive notice from the land records does not prevent A–2 from becoming a holder in due course. *See* UCC § 3–302(b). However, authority to the contrary exists.

Illustration: MR executes a negotiable note and a mortgage to ME. ME sells the loan to A–1. ME negotiates the note and assigns the mortgage to A–1 who takes possession of the documents, but does not record the mortgage assignment. ME then sells and assigns the documents to A–2 who relies on the land records, but, of course, does not receive the documents. A–1 and A–2 each claim ownership of the note and the mortgage. Under the generally held view, A–1 prevails because A–2 is not a *holder* in due course and therefore, takes subject to A–1's claim of legal title.

B.   UCC ARTICLE 9 APPROACH

Article 9 of the UCC resolves the conflict among assignees by providing that typically whoever takes possession of the mortgage note prevails. Specifically, UCC § 9–330(d) states that the "purchaser of an instrument has priority over a security interest in the instrument protected by a method other than possession if the purchaser gives value and takes possession of the instrument in good faith and without knowledge that the purchase violates the rights of the secured party." *But see* UCC § 9–331(a)(noting exceptions). The purchaser is considered to have knowledge-of-violation if the note bears notice of the prior assignment. *See* UCC § 9–330(f).

VI. FRACTIONAL ASSIGNMENTS (LOAN PARTICIPATION)

A. FORMS OF LOAN PARTICIPATION

Mortgagees commonly assign fractional interests in large mortgage loans to other investors. This technique is referred to as loan participation. *See* Ch. 2, p. 27 (discussing loan participation). A loan participation is normally structured in either of two ways. (1) The mortgagee takes a single mortgage note from the mortgagor, holds it, and issues participation certificates to the investors. (2) The mortgagee takes a series of notes from the mortgagor, each note for a fraction of the mortgage debt. The mortgagee then assigns some of the notes to the investors.

Although the series-of-notes method of participation was formerly quite common, today the certificate approach is employed extensively. In either case, priority problems arise when the foreclosure sale proceeds are insufficient to pay all the investors.

B. AGREEMENT ESTABLISHING PRIORITY

Most modern participations are governed by a separate participation agreement that establishes priority among the parties. (An agreement regarding priority, of course, could be included in the mortgage.) The agreement ordinarily provides that all investors, including the mortgagee, have equal priority and share ratably in the foreclosure sale proceeds.

C.   PRIORITY ABSENT AGREEMENT— PARTICIPATION CERTIFICATES

Each loan participant's interest is usually represented by a participation certificate. As previously indicated, priority among the investors is almost invariably covered by a participation agreement. In the rare instances where no agreement exists, the pro rata rule applies because the certificates do not purport to assign any specific part of the mortgage loan. Thus, absent an agreement to the contrary, all investors, including the mortgagee, hold undivided interests having equal priority.

An exception to this rule exists. If the mortgagor guarantees payment of a certificate, the certificate holder is given priority over the mortgagee on the ground the guaranty indicates the intent to grant the certificate holder a superior claim.

D.   PRIORITY ABSENT AGREEMENT— SERIES OF NOTES

Participations originally involved the assignment of a series of notes. The parties to these participations often failed to make provision in the mortgage for priority among the holders of the notes.

Absent such an agreement, the courts were forced to develop principles governing the allocation of foreclosure sale proceeds. A tangle of conflicting rules and exceptions resulted.

1.   Pro Rata Rule

The general rule is that, absent agreement fixing priority, the mortgage is enforced on a pro rata basis in favor of the mortgagee and all assignees. This rule is predicated on the theory that equality is equity.

> *Illustration*: MR executes five $1,000 promissory notes and a mortgage to ME. ME sells and assigns one note to each A, B, C, and D. ME retains one note. The parties make no agreement regarding the priority of their interests. MR defaults, and a foreclosure sale produces $2,000. Under the pro rata rule each ME, A, B, C, and D is entitled to ⅕ of the $2,000 proceeds ($400).

a.   Guaranty Exception

Courts in most pro rata states make an exception to the general rule when the mortgagee assigns a note with a guaranty of payment. In such case, the assignee is normally awarded priority over the mortgagee on the theory that the assignee has the greater equity.

b.   Priority–for–Assignees Exception

In a few pro rata jurisdictions, the general rule is not available to the mortgagee. The note or notes that the mortgagee retains are postponed in priority to those held by the assignees.

Illustration: Assume the same fact situation as in the immediately preceding illustration. In a state that applies the pro rata rule only to assignees, A, B, C, and D have a $4,000 first lien as a group, and ME has a $1,000 second lien. Each assignee receives ¼ of the $2,000 proceeds obtained at foreclosure ($500). ME recovers nothing because the proceeds are not sufficient to pay off the assignees' $4,000 first lien.

Priority for assignees is justified on a variety of equitable grounds that have a common source—the theory that assignment of part of the debt operates also as a pro tanto assignment of the mortgage lien. Thus, the priority-for-assignees exception to the pro rata rule is sometimes inaccurately referred to as the pro tanto rule. The label is misleading because the pro tanto assignment concept is applied only between the mortgagee and the assignees. The assignees themselves share pro rata. The priority-for-assignees exception is, therefore, at most a severely limited pro tanto approach. As discussed below, the true pro tanto rule establishes priority among assignees in the order they acquire their notes.

c.   *Order-of-Maturity Exception*

Some pro rata states do not apply the general rule if the mortgage debt is represented by a series of notes having different dates of maturity. In these states, priority is awarded the parties in the order of maturity of their notes.

Illustration: MR executes to ME a series of three $1,000 promissory notes: #1 matures in one year, #2 matures in two years, and #3 matures in three years. The notes are all secured by a single mortgage. ME sells and assigns note #1 to A and note #2 to B. The parties make no agreement regarding the priority of their interests. MR defaults, and a foreclosure sale produces $1,500. Under the order-of-maturity exception, A receives $1,000, B receives $500, and ME receives nothing.

2. Priority of Assignment Rule (Pro Tanto Rule)

A few jurisdictions reject the pro rata rule with its various exceptions in favor of the principle that, absent agreement to the contrary, assignees have priority in the order the assignments were made. This approach, known as the priority of assignment rule or the pro tanto rule, is based on the theory that each assignee receives that portion of the mortgage necessary to secure the interest assigned. Under this approach, subsequent participants take subject to the rights of prior assignees, and the mortgagee takes subject to all.

Illustration: MR executes to ME a series of three $1,000 promissory notes maturing in three successive years. The notes are secured by a single mortgage. ME assigns one of the notes to A and then assigns another note to B. ME retains one note. The parties make no agreement regarding the priority of their notes. MR defaults, and foreclosure sale produces $1,500. Under the pro tanto rule, A receives

$1,000, B gets $500, and ME receives nothing. The maturity dates of the notes are irrelevant.

VII. ASSIGNMENT BY OPERATION OF LAW (SUBROGATION)

Courts may imply an assignment of the mortgage by operation of law under the equitable doctrine of subrogation. In real estate finance law, subrogation is the substitution of one who pays the mortgage debt to the position of the mortgagee.

A. PARTIES FOR WHOM SUBROGATION IS AVAILABLE

A payor who is neither the primary obligor nor a mere volunteer may be subrogated to the rights of the mortgagee. (The primary obligor and the volunteer are not eligible for subrogation because they have no compelling equities in their favor.) Following are situations in which the payor commonly qualifies for this form of equitable relief.

1. Mortgagor as Surety After Conveyance

Upon conveying away the mortgaged real estate subject to the mortgage, the mortgagor becomes a surety. *See* Ch. 6, pp. 113–121 (discussing rights and obligations of parties when mortgage survives conveyance). If the grantee fails to pay the obligation and the mortgagor is forced to do so, justice demands that the mortgagor be subrogated to the rights of the mortgagee.

Illustration: MR executes a promissory note and a mortgage to ME. MR sells and conveys the mortgaged property to GE subject to the mortgage. GE fails to pay the obligation, so MR as surety pays ME. MR is thereby subrogated to ME's right to foreclose. If GE assumed the obligation, MR also receives ME's right to recover a deficiency judgment against GE.

2.   Junior Mortgagee

When a junior mortgagee pays off a prior lien for the protection of its own security interest, it is subrogated to the rights of the mortgagee receiving payment.

Illustration: MR executes a $10,000 promissory note and a mortgage to ME–1. MR then executes a $5,000 note and a second mortgage on the same land to ME–2. MR becomes insolvent and defaults on both obligations. Property values have recently slumped, and it is projected that a foreclosure sale will produce only $10,000. Because ME–2 will receive nothing in that case, ME–2 desires to postpone foreclosure. ME–2, therefore, pays ME–1 and is subrogated to ME–1's rights. The land remains subject to two liens, both in favor of ME–2 who can wait until property values rise to foreclose.

3.   Lender of Pay-Off Funds

One who loans funds to pay off an existing mortgage may be subrogated to the rights of the mortgagee receiving payment.

Illustration: MR executes a promissory note and a mortgage to ME. MR obtains a loan from L to pay off ME and executes a new promissory note and mortgage to L. MR uses the loan proceeds to pay ME. L's mortgage, however, is defective for some reason. L is subrogated to ME's lien rights in order to cure the defect and give L the security for which L bargained.

Illustration: ME–1 holds a first mortgage on MR's land, and ME–2 holds a second mortgage. MR borrows money from L to pay off ME–1. L is ignorant of ME–2's mortgage even though it is recorded. MR executes a promissory note and a mortgage to L. MR uses the loan proceeds to pay ME–1. L then discovers ME–2's mortgage lien. Courts following the generally accepted view subrogate L to ME–1's priority position on the theory that equity demands it and ME–2 is not prejudiced. (Indeed a growing number of decisions, fueled by the Restatement (Third) of Property— Mortgages, reach the same result when L actually knows of ME–2's mortgage, notwithstanding the traditional rule to the contrary. *See* Bank of America, N.A. v. Prestance Corporation, 160 P.3d 17 (Wash. 2007).) Some courts, however, refuse to apply the doctrine of subrogation because L's loss was the result of L's own negligence in failing to check the records. Sometimes a line is drawn between ordinary negligence and unjustifiable negligence.

4. Purchaser of Mortgaged Property

When a purchaser of the mortgaged property assumes and pays the mortgage debt under the mistaken belief that no junior encumbrances exist, the purchaser may be subrogated to the rights of the mortgagee. There is, however, a division of opinion on the question.

> *Illustration*: MR owns land subject to a first mortgage to ME–1 and a second mortgage to ME–2. MR sells and conveys the land to GE who assumes the obligation to ME–1. GE is ignorant of ME–2's mortgage even though it is recorded. If GE pays ME–1, many courts will subrogate GE to ME–1's priority position in order to prevent the gratuitous advancement of ME–2's lien priority. Other courts, however, deny subrogation for various reasons, including the notion that GE is now the primary obligor, a party for whom subrogation is unavailable.

B. CONVENTIONAL SUBROGATION

The mortgagor and the payor sometimes enter an agreement that subrogation should occur in the payor's favor. Although subrogation consistent with this agreement is called conventional subrogation, the actual legal effect of the agreement is subject to dispute. Some courts treat conventional subrogation as solely contractual in nature and, therefore, separate from equitable subrogation. (Equitable subrogation is sometimes referred to as legal subrogation.) Many courts, however, view the agreement calling for subrogation as merely an important factor that often influences equity to act to prevent injustice in individual cases.

Illustration: MR obtains a construction loan from ME and executes a promissory note and a mortgage to ME. During the course of construction, M performs work on the project, but is not paid. Under local law, M may file a mechanics' lien on the property within ninety days after completion of the project. The lien will relate back to when construction began. *See* Ch. 9, pp. 192–196 (analyzing mechanics' lien statutes). ME's construction loan mortgage was recorded prior to commencement of construction and thus, under local law has priority over all mechanics' liens. Sixty days after completion of construction, P makes a permanent mortgage loan to MR to "take-out" ME's construction mortgage loan. *See* Ch. 2, pp. 13–14 (discussing relationship between construction lenders and permanent lenders). MR executes a new promissory note and mortgage to P who is justifiably ignorant of M's claim. The mortgage contains a provision that P is subrogated to any lien discharged by proceeds of P's loan. Eighty days after completion of construction, M records a mechanics' lien that relates back to the beginning of construction and therefore, is prior to the lien of P's mortgage. P, however, is subrogated to ME's priority position. This conclusion may be reached on various grounds. One approach is that subrogation is enforced as a contractual right. Another view is that subrogation occurs by operation of law and that the existence of the agreement merely indicates P is entitled to equitable relief.

C. RIGHT TO FORMAL ASSIGNMENT

A subrogee usually may compel the mortgagee to formally assign the obligation and the mortgage.

VIII. ASSIGNMENT AS SECURITY

The mortgagee may assign the note and mortgage as security for a loan received by the mortgagee. *See* Ch. 5, pp. 102–103 (discussing mortgageable interests). Such collateral assignments are common practice, notably among mortgage bankers who frequently employ this technique to obtain financing. *See* Ch. 2, pp. 22–23 (discussing mortgage banking companies and mortgage warehousing).

A lender that takes a collateral assignment of a note and mortgage may perfect its security interest against the mortgagee's future lien creditors and bankruptcy trustee by filing pursuant to the requirements of UCC Article 9. *See* UCC §§ 9–312(a), 9–317(a). A collateral assignee, however, must obtain possession of the note, or place notice of the assignment on the note, to be shielded from claims of subsequent ordinary or collateral assignees of the mortgage loan. *See* UCC § 9–330(d) & (f). *See also* pp. 149–150 (discussing UCC Article 9 approach to conflicting assignments). Under the theory that the mortgage travels with the note, recording in the land records is not required, indeed is insufficient, to protect the collateral assignee's security rights in the mortgage vis-à-vis the potential claimants noted above. *See* UCC §§ 9–109(b); 9–308(e). Nonetheless, the prudent collateral assignee will record the assignment for other purposes, such as to prevent improper release of the mortgage. *See* pp. 135–137 (analyzing recording mortgage assignment).

IX. TRANSFER AT MORTGAGEE'S DEATH

The mortgagee's interest in the mortgage loan passes as personal property at the mortgagee's death on the theory that the mortgage, the realty aspect of the mortgage loan, is merely an incident of the obligation, the personalty aspect. This rule is, however, of waning significance. Two reasons exist for its decline in importance. First, most mortgagees are institutions that may last in perpetuity. Second, even when the mortgagee is an individual, modern intestacy statutes generally provide that personalty and realty descend in the same way.

CHAPTER 8

AFTER DEFAULT AND BEFORE FORECLOSURE

I. DEFAULT

A. DEFINITION AND SIGNIFICANCE OF DEFAULT

Default occurs when the mortgagor fails to pay the underlying debt or to perform some other obligation secured by the mortgage. What constitutes default in each case, therefore, can be determined only by examining the mortgage loan documents in question.

Default activates a set of mortgage law principles that determine the rights and obligations of the mortgagor and the mortgagee until foreclosure occurs. This chapter is devoted to an analysis of these principles. *See also* Ch. 4, p. 98 (discussing default interest).

B. COMMON TYPES OF DEFAULT

1. Failure to Pay Principal and Interest

Most defaults occur as a result of the mortgagor's failure to pay monthly installments of principal and interest.

2. Failure to Pay Taxes or Insurance

The mortgagor's failure to pay real estate taxes or insurance premiums once were common types of default. The use of escrow accounts, however, has reduced the frequency of default in these areas. *See* Ch. 4, pp. 96–98 (treating escrow accounts).

3. Waste

Mortgages commonly provide that the commission of waste on the mortgaged property constitutes default. *See* Ch. 5, pp. 108–110 (discussing waste of mortgaged property).

4. Construction Difficulties

Construction mortgages present additional possibilities for breach. Default often occurs because the mortgagor is unable to complete the contemplated improvements in accordance with the terms of the construction loan agreement. *See* Ch. 2, pp. 14–16 (analyzing construction lender's special risks).

C. WAIVER OF DEFAULT

The mortgagee may waive default by accepting late payment or other tardy performance. Lenders usually are willing to make some allowance for the borrower's financial difficulties because a modicum of tolerance often reaps greater monetary return than hasty invocation of expensive and protracted foreclosure procedures. *See* Ch. 10, pp. 211–223 (discussing foreclosure process).

Waiver of one late performance traditionally has not been viewed as constituting waiver of subsequent late performances. Some courts, however, may require a mortgagee who has regularly accepted late performance to give the mortgagor notice of its intention to require timely performance in the future. Many mortgages address this subject by providing that forbearance does not constitute waiver. Clauses permitting the mortgagee to assess a charge for late payment also are common. *See* Ch. 4, p. 98 (considering late charges).

II. ACCELERATION

A. ACCELERATION CLAUSE

One of the most significant provisions in the modern amortized mortgage is the clause that authorizes the mortgagee to accelerate the entire debt when the mortgagor defaults in the payment of a single monthly installment or in the performance of any other obligation secured by the mortgage. Without an acceleration clause, the mortgagee can institute foreclosure proceedings to recover only the amount in default. *See* Ch. 10, pp. 211–223 (discussing foreclosure process). Further, if the mortgagee does foreclose in such a situation, authorities are in conflict as to whether the lien for the amount not in default survives foreclosure.

Illustration: MR executes a $40,000 promissory note and a mortgage to ME. The documents provide for equal monthly payments of $300 over a thirty-year term, but do not include an acceleration clause. MR misses two payments. ME may institute foreclosure proceedings, but is only entitled to that part of the proceeds sufficient to satisfy the partial default ($600). In some states, the mortgage lien continues on the property to secure the unpaid balance of the debt. Any surplus goes to the mortgagor. In other jurisdictions, however, the property is sold free from the mortgage lien. In such case, the surplus is usually either applied immediately to the unpaid balance of the loan or placed in trust to cover the debt as it matures.

An acceleration clause should be included in both the note and the mortgage. These clauses should coincide in all respects. In this regard, the note may refer to the mortgage for acceleration rights. The note's negotiability is not affected by such reference. *See* UCC § 3–106(b). *See also* Ch. 4, pp. 75–76 (discussing form of obligation).

If an acceleration clause is included only in the mortgage, the mortgagee may experience difficulty in accelerating the loan. Authorities are divided concerning the significance of its omission from the note. One view is that the mortgagee can accelerate under both documents on the theory that the note and mortgage are integral components of a single contract. The other view is that the mortgagee can only accelerate under the mortgage.

Illustration: MR executes a promissory note and a mortgage to ME. An acceleration clause is included in the mortgage, but is omitted from the note. MR defaults by failing to make two monthly payments. ME can accelerate under the mortgage, foreclose, and apply the foreclosure sale proceeds to the entire debt. In some states, ME also can obtain a deficiency judgment against MR on the note. In others, ME cannot.

B. CURING DEFAULT BEFORE ACCELERATION

The mortgagor may reinstate the mortgage loan by curing default before the mortgagee accelerates.

Illustration: MR executes a promissory note and a mortgage to ME. The documents contain identical acceleration clauses. MR defaults by missing one monthly payment. If MR makes late payment to ME before ME accelerates, the loan is reinstated. ME may not use the cured default as a basis for acceleration. ME, of course, may accelerate after a later default.

Today, residential mortgages often provide that, with certain exceptions, the mortgagee must give the mortgagor notice of impending acceleration and the opportunity to avoid it by curing default.

C. TRIGGERING ACCELERATION

Acceleration clauses are usually activated at the mortgagee's option. A self-operating clause could result in acceleration contrary to the mortgagee's best interest. Optional acceleration is triggered by the mortgagee's performance of an act that clearly evidences the intent to treat the entire debt as due. In most states, formal notice of acceleration is unnecessary. The filing of a foreclosure complaint is generally sufficient to indicate an election to accelerate.

D. CURING DEFAULT AFTER ACCELERATION

1. General Rule

The general rule is that after the mortgagee accelerates, the mortgagor cannot reinstate the loan by curing the original default. The mortgagor must pay the entire debt or face foreclosure. However, several state legislatures have enacted statutes that permit mortgagors to nullify acceleration by paying just the amount originally in default. Moreover, some commonly used mortgage forms give the mortgagor a similar contract right.

2. Equitable Relief

Mortgagors occasionally seek to have an acceleration set aside on the ground that the default which triggered it resulted from misunderstanding or excusable neglect. Equitable relief is commonly unavailable in such cases. Many courts view an acceleration clause as an agreement regarding the time for payment whose enforcement does not exact a penalty or involve a forfeiture. Thus, the mortgagee may enforce the clause as written unless it has acted fraudulently, unconscionably, or in bad faith. A contrary view, however, exists. In an increasing number of jurisdictions, courts refuse to recognize an acceleration that would produce inequity or injustice.

   Illustration: MR executes a promissory note and a mortgage to ME. The documents contain identical optional acceleration clauses. MR goes to Europe on business, but advises an assistant to make the next required payment to ME. MR's assistant uses the wrong mathematical formula to compute the interest and therefore, pays a little less than is due. ME elects to accelerate and foreclose because of this minor default. MR returns from Europe, makes late tender of the unpaid interest, and requests the court to set aside the acceleration. In many states, courts will not grant relief for breach of contract resulting from MR's negligence. *See* Graf v. Hope Building Corporation, 171 N.E. 884 (N.Y.1930). The trend, however, is to grant MR relief when acceleration is inequitable or unjust under the circumstances. Although MR's willingness to cure the default is not sufficient reason to grant equitable relief under this emerging view, other factors, such as MR's good faith and the unusual situation, indicate that the acceleration should be set aside. *See* Federal Home Loan Mortgage Corporation v. Taylor, 318 So.2d 203 (Fla.App.1975).

E.   DUE–ON–SALE CLAUSE

Mortgages often provide for acceleration if the mortgagor transfers any interest in the mortgaged property without the mortgagee's consent. These due-on-sale clauses present special legal problems that are discussed in an earlier chapter. *See* Ch. 6, pp. 123–130 (analyzing due-on-sale clause).

III.   RIGHT TO POSSESSION AND RENTS

A.   SIGNIFICANCE OF MORTGAGE THEORIES

Title, intermediate, and lien mortgage theories are significant today primarily as they relate to possession of the mortgaged real estate. *See* Ch. 1, pp. 8–10 (discussing mortgage theories). Possession is important because with it comes the right to rents and profits produced by the property.

A basic tenet of common law is that possession is an attribute of legal title. Thus, in title theory states, the mortgagee receives the right to possession when the mortgage is executed. In intermediate theory jurisdictions, the mortgagee ostensibly receives legal "title," but is allowed by law to take possession only upon default. In lien theory states, the mortgagee does not receive title of any kind and, therefore, generally cannot take possession at any time, even after default.

The confusion created by these conflicting theories has been somewhat alleviated by the common practice of dealing with the issue of possession in the mortgage contract itself. The modern mortgage often provides that the mortgagor has the right to possession until default and the mortgagee has the right thereafter. Courts in some lien theory states, however, refuse to enforce mortgage agreements of this type for public policy reasons. But even in those jurisdictions, the mortgagor may give possession to the mortgagee after default.

Hence, as a practical matter, default frequently gives the mortgagee the right to possession either by operation of law or by mortgage provision. The consequences of this right are explored in the next section.

B.   MORTGAGEE IN POSSESSION

1.   Definition

When the mortgagee lawfully exercises dominion and control over the mortgaged property pursuant to the mortgage, it is known as a mortgagee in possession. A mortgagee may take possession without physically entering or occupying the property, so long as it exercises substantially the same control as the mortgagor normally would exert.

> *Illustration*: MR executes a mortgage on a vacant farm to ME. The mortgage authorizes ME to take possession upon default. MR defaults. ME need not actually occupy the farm to become a mortgagee in possession. Maintaining the property and seeking tenants would be sufficient.

2.   Rights

A mortgagee in possession may control the property until either redemption or foreclosure occurs and collect all rents and profits arising from the land during that time. The mortgagee, of course, does not acquire title to the mortgaged real estate merely by taking possession of it under the mortgage.

3. Obligations

All states impose trustee-like obligations on a mortgagee in possession.

a. *Management*

A mortgagee in possession must manage and maintain the property in a prudent manner and apply receipts in excess of costs to the mortgage debt. The obligation of prudent management requires that a mortgagee in possession use reasonable efforts to make the property productive. The mortgagee is, therefore, chargeable for rent it could have secured but for lack of reasonable diligence. And, if the mortgagee occupies the property for its own use, it is generally accountable for the fair rental value of its occupancy without regard to whether the property produces more or less than that amount.

b. *Accounting*

A mortgagee in possession does not act free from judicial scrutiny. The mortgagor can require the mortgagee to make a detailed accounting of receipts and expenses, but only in a foreclosure action or upon redemption.

c. *Liability to Third Parties*

A mortgagee in possession may incur liabilities to third parties. The mortgagee is responsible in tort for its negligence in managing the mortgaged real estate and in contract for goods and services properly supplied to the property during the mortgagee's possession.

4. Problem of Leases Existing at Default

When mortgaged property is subject to a lease at the time of default, a mortgagee who has the right to take possession either by law or by agreement can ascertain its rights and duties vis-à-vis the lessee only by determining whether the lease was made before or after the execution of the mortgage. It is assumed in the following discussion that all instruments were promptly recorded, so that the order of their execution is also the order of their priority under applicable recording statutes. *See* Ch. 9, pp. 186–187 (discussing recording statutes).

a. Prior Leases

If the lease was executed before the mortgage, the mortgagee in possession is bound by the lease because the mortgagee's security extends only to the interest the mortgagor owned at the time the mortgage was created. The lessee under a prior lease is also bound because the mortgagee in possession succeeds to the mortgagor's reversion and thereby establishes privity of estate. Hence, the lessee may remain on the property, but must pay rent to the mortgagee in possession.

b. Junior Leases

If the lease was executed after the mortgage, the mortgagee may take possession and thereby terminate the lease on the theory that the lessee can have no greater right to possession than the lessor. Although the mortgagee appears to be in a generally favorable position in this situation, it is really at an advantage only if it desires to terminate the junior lease. If the mortgagee wants to continue the junior lease and collect rent from the junior lessee, difficulty arises because the lessee is liable only to one with whom the lessee is in either privity of contract or privity of estate. The junior lessee clearly has no contractual obligation to the mortgagee. In addition, no privity of estate exists between the junior lessee and the mortgagee because the mortgage could not transfer the mortgagor's reversion against a lessee not then in existence. The mortgagee, therefore, faces "Catch 22" of real estate finance law. Because the mortgagee cannot force the junior lessee to enter a contract, the mortgagee is entitled to receive rent only if it can establish privity of estate with the lessee. If, however, the mortgagee attempts to do so by taking possession, the junior lease and the lessee's obligations thereunder are destroyed on the ground that the mortgagee's possession relates back to when the mortgage was executed.

The mortgagee in possession may avoid this dilemma by persuading the junior lessee to enter an attornment agreement recognizing the mortgagee as lessor. This arrangement establishes the privity of contract necessary for the mortgagee to enforce the lease. The attornment agreement is in reality a new lease. Hence, the lessee and the mortgagee in possession may choose to set entirely new terms.

Although some junior lessees attorn to a mortgagee in possession, others take advantage of the situation to rid themselves of what they consider to be an undesirable lease. This may be disastrous to the mortgagee who was depending upon their rents to pay the mortgage debt.

The mortgagee, therefore, should take steps to insure that it can preserve and enforce junior leases after default. Several options are available. First, the mortgagee could subordinate the mortgage to junior leases so that they would be treated as prior leases and therefore, survive the mortgagee's possession as well as foreclosure. *See* Ch. 9, pp. 190–195 (discussing subordination agreements). Second, the mortgagee could require the mortgagor to negotiate an attornment provision in each valuable junior lease whereby the junior lessee agrees to recognize the mortgagee as landlord if the lessor-mortgagor defaults on the mortgage. The lessee, of course, may seek to have the mortgagee execute a non-disturbance agreement in return. (Such a combination of attornment and non-disturbance agreements may be employed to maintain a junior lease beyond foreclosure.) Third, the mortgagee could require that the mortgagor assign rents generated by the mortgaged property, an alternative explored in the following section. Fourth, after default the mortgagee could seek the appointment of a receiver of rents, a course of action that is discussed later in this chapter.

C. ASSIGNMENT OF RENTS

The mortgagee may require the mortgagor to execute an assignment of rents giving the mortgagee an interest in all present and future leases and in all rents issuing from the mortgaged real estate independent of any right the mortgagee may have to take possession of the property. The practical effect of an assignment of rents is that upon default the mortgagee, as assignee of the mortgagor's rights, may collect rents without taking possession under the mortgage. Thus, the mortgagee can preserve and enforce junior leases until foreclosure. Moreover, in most jurisdictions the mortgagee may establish the priority of its interest in rents over subsequent claimants by recording the assignment, without taking any step to activate it. In certain states, however, priority dates from activation on the ground that the assignment is "inchoate" before then.

A division of opinion exists as to how an assignment of rents may be activated so that the mortgagee can begin collecting rents. The precise language of the assignment may be determinative. There is authority that an assignment of rents is an "absolute" assignment triggered automatically upon default. However, the generally accepted view is that an assignment of rents constitutes a security interest that the mortgagee must trigger by taking some affirmative step after default. The type of action required varies among the states. Depending upon the jurisdiction, the mortgagee may activate the assignment of rents by making formal demand of the mortgagor, by giving notice to the lessees, by filing a foreclosure suit seeking the appointment of a receiver, by taking possession of the property, or by obtaining the appointment of a receiver.

An assignment of rents also protects the mortgagee from being bound by agreements for advance rental payment, rent reduction, or lease cancellation commonly used by mortgagors in distress to milk the mortgaged property of all potential revenue. If the mortgagee obtains an assignment of rents, records it, and gives notice to existing lessees, all lessees enter advance payment, rent reduction, and cancellation agreements with the mortgagor at their peril.

The National Conference of Commissioners on Uniform State Laws sought to reconstruct the fragmented assignment-of-rents legal framework by crafting the Uniform Assignment of Rents Act. This 2005 measure has been enacted in just one state.

D. RECEIVER

1. Background

The mortgagee may seek to have a receiver for rents and profits appointed in an action for foreclosure. This is a particularly valuable option in lien theory states where the mortgagee cannot obtain possession and reach rents and profits absent the mortgagor's agreement that the mortgagee may do so.

Even when the mortgagee has the right to possession of the mortgaged real estate upon default, it may want to have a receiver appointed rather than take possession itself. Several reasons support such an approach. First, the stringent accounting duties imposed on a mortgagee in possession are avoided. Second, the potential tort and contract liabilities of a mortgagee in possession are eliminated. Third, junior leases are preserved and rents may be collected under those leases even when there is no assignment of rents.

2.   Grounds for Appointment

A receivership is an equitable remedy designed to preserve the mortgaged property pending foreclosure. The appointment of a receiver is generally within the court's sound discretion bounded only by the traditional requirement that due consideration be given to the security's adequacy, the existence or likelihood of waste, and the mortgagor's financial position. Judicial authority in this area has been further broadened by the common use of a mortgage clause authorizing the mortgagee to obtain the appointment of a receiver.

Courts have exercised their largely unbridled discretion in markedly different ways. In a number of states, the appointment of a receiver is virtually automatic upon request. Indeed, such a result is dictated by statute in certain jurisdictions when the mortgage contains a receivership clause. Residing at the opposite end of the spectrum are states in which a receiver is appointed only in the most compelling circumstances. The bulk of jurisdictions take various positions somewhere between these polar approaches.

3. Receiver's Powers

Once appointed, the receiver generally is empowered to preserve the mortgagee's security by taking possession of the mortgaged real estate and collecting rents and profits. Although an exhaustive analysis of a receiver's authority is beyond the scope of these materials, certain areas of receiver action deserve additional discussion.

a. Collecting Rent From Junior Lessees

A mortgagee may utilize a receiver to reach rent payable under a lease entered after the execution of the mortgage even when there is no assignment of rents. The receiver's action is that of the court, not the mortgagee, so it does not automatically destroy junior leases.

b. Collecting Rent From Mortgagor in Residence

A vexing rent collection problem arises when the mortgagor occupies the mortgaged property as a residence. Although some authority exists that a receiver may collect rent from the mortgagor in such cases, courts may be hesitant to permit a receiver to do so. *See* Holmes v. Gravenhorst, 188 N.E. 285 (N.Y.1933).

c. Operating Mortgagor's Business

Mortgagees may request the appointment of a receiver to operate the mortgagor's business pending foreclosure. A court generally will grant the request only if the business is either specifically covered by the mortgage or based primarily on the rental value of the mortgaged real estate, as in the case of an apartment building.

IV. EQUITY OF REDEMPTION

A. AVAILABILITY

Certain qualified individuals may prevent foreclosure by paying off the mortgage debt before the completion of foreclosure proceedings. *See* Ch. 10, pp. 211–223 (discussing foreclosure process). This right of late payment is known as the equity of redemption. *See* Ch. 1, pp. 4–5 (tracing evolution of equity of redemption).

B. PARTIES WHO MAY REDEEM

The mortgagor, of course, may redeem. In addition, any party acquiring an interest in, or a lien on, the mortgaged property after the attachment of the mortgage may redeem because its interest will be cut off by foreclosure. Eligible redemptioners include grantees, heirs, devisees, junior lessees, and junior encumbrancers. When several parties have equitable redemption rights, they may redeem in the order of the priority of their interests, subject to the mortgagor's ultimate right to redeem.

C.   AMOUNT REQUIRED
FOR REDEMPTION

Equitable redemption generally can be accomplished only by paying the entire mortgage debt. However, in the event that the entire debt is not in default, as in the case of an unaccelerated amortized loan, the mortgagor may reinstate the loan and avoid foreclosure by making late payment of the overdue amount. In the following discussion it is assumed that the entire mortgage debt is in default.

D.   RESULT OF REDEMPTION

1.   By Mortgagor or Mortgagor's Successor

Redemption by the mortgagor or the mortgagor's successor discharges the mortgage lien. Junior interests survive unless also paid off.

2.   By Junior Interest Holder

Redemption by a junior interest holder does not terminate the mortgage from which the property is redeemed. On the contrary, the mortgage survives, and the one who redeems is subrogated to the rights of the mortgagee. *See* Ch. 7, pp. 155–160 (discussing subrogation).

> *Illustration*: MR executes a $10,000 first mortgage to ME–1, then a $5,000 second mortgage to ME–2, and finally a $2,000 third mortgage to ME–3. MR defaults on all loans, and each mortgagee accelerates. MR may pay ME–1 $10,000 and free the land from the first mortgage. In that

case, the second and third mortgage liens would remain. ME–2 also may pay ME–1 $10,000 before MR does so. This would not terminate the first mortgage. All three mortgages would remain, but now ME–2 would hold both the first and second mortgages. ME–3 could then redeem from ME–2 by paying ME–2 the total amount of the first and second liens ($15,000). This would not terminate either the first or second mortgages. All three mortgages would remain, but they now would be held by ME–3. MR has the ultimate right to redeem. MR, however, must pay ME–3 the total of all mortgage liens ($17,000) to redeem the land free from encumbrances.

E.   ENFORCEMENT OF RIGHT TO REDEEM

If the parties cannot agree on the question of redemption, the one asserting a right to redeem may file a bill in equity to enforce this right.

F.   WAIVER/CLOGGING

Courts will not recognize mortgage clauses that waive or otherwise clog the mortgagor's equity of redemption. *See* Ch. 1, p. 5 (discussing preservation/clogging equity of redemption).

G. WHEN RIGHT OF REDEMPTION ENDS

1. Foreclosure

The completion of foreclosure terminates the equity of redemption of all parties defendant. If foreclosure is by judicial sale, the right to redeem generally ends when the court confirms the sale. If foreclosure is by power of sale, the right to redeem ends when the sale is final under local law.

A junior interest holder omitted from the foreclosure proceedings retains both the junior interest and an equity of redemption. The omitted junior interest holder, therefore, may seek to assert the right to redeem even after foreclosure. *See* Ch. 10, p. 215 (analyzing rights of omitted junior lienor).

2. Termination by Other Means

A mortgagor's equitable right to redeem may be barred by estoppel, laches, or a statute of limitations. Generally, none of these possibilities will arise if the mortgagor remains on the mortgaged property. It is when the mortgagee takes possession that circumstances are ripe for the development of these bars to redemption.

V. ALTERNATIVES TO FORECLOSURE

Although a mortgagee is entitled to commence foreclosure proceedings after default, it may decide to pursue another course of action initially.

A. WORKOUT ARRANGEMENT

Institutional mortgage lenders desire to avoid foreclosure. Their business is to obtain a reasonable return on their investments, not to engage in litigation. Consequently, they often lower monthly payments, extend the time for payment, waive late charges, or make any other reasonable arrangement that allows the mortgagor to work out of temporary financial difficulty.

B. DEED IN LIEU OF FORECLOSURE

If the mortgagor cannot possibly pay the mortgage obligation, the mortgagee may be willing to accept a deed to the mortgaged real estate in lieu of foreclosure. *See* Ch. 6, p. 122 (discussing deed in lieu of foreclosure).

C. SALE/"SHORT SALE"

A mortgagor in default may decide to sell the mortgaged real estate and satisfy the mortgage loan with the proceeds of the sale. See Ch. 6, pp. 111–113 (discussing mortgagor's power to convey and effect of conveyance on mortgage). If, however, the balance of the mortgage loan exceeds the market value of the realty, this route to discharging the loan is seemingly unavailable. Nonetheless, a mortgagee may agree to a "short sale" in such a situation. As a general matter, a "short sale" arrangement involves selling the property at a price lower than the outstanding mortgage debt, applying the sale proceeds to reduce the debt, cancelling the obligation that remains or establishing terms for its full or partial repayment, and releasing the mortgage.

D.   RECOVERY ON THE NOTE ALONE/"ONE ACTION" RULE

Even if litigation is necessary, the mortgagee generally may sue on the note without foreclosing the mortgage. This principle is predicated on the notion that because the underlying obligation is the essential element of the transaction, the mortgagee may treat the note as unsecured if it so wishes. In California and a few other states, however, the mortgagee's only remedy on default is to foreclose and obtain a deficiency judgment if appropriate. *See* Ch. 10, pp. 216–217, 219–220 (discussing deficiency judgment). This "one action" rule is based on the theory that because the mortgaged property is the primary fund for repayment of the debt, the mortgagee must exhaust it before seeking satisfaction from the mortgagor's other assets. The rule also is designed to protect the mortgagor from multiple actions arising from the same loan transaction.

Where suit on the note alone is permitted, the mortgage is not affected by the resulting personal judgment against the mortgagor. The debt merges into the judgment, and the judgment becomes the underlying obligation. Whatever the mortgagee then collects from the mortgagor's other assets is credited against this obligation. The only significant change in the legal relationship of the parties is that enforcement of the underlying obligation is now governed by the statute of limitations on judgments rather than by the statute of limitations on promissory notes.

CHAPTER 9

PRIORITIES

I. GENERAL PRINCIPLES

When foreclosure is imminent, the mortgagee and other parties holding interests in the mortgaged property become particularly concerned about the priority of their respective interests. Their concern is well founded. First, interests acquired before the mortgage survive foreclosure; those acquired after the mortgage are extinguished. *See* Ch. 10, pp. 207–208 (analyzing availability and purpose of foreclosure). Second, the mortgagee and subsequent interest holders are paid from the proceeds of the foreclosure sale in the order of their priority, and the proceeds may be insufficient to pay everyone. *See* Ch. 10, pp. 216, 219–220 (discussing distribution of proceeds).

II. RECORDING STATUTES

The principle "prior in time, prior in right" determines the order of priority among interest holders in the mortgaged property unless a subsequent purchaser fits within the protection afforded by the local recording statute. Recording statutes vary with regard to the requirements that a subsequent purchaser must meet. Depending on the jurisdiction, a subsequent purchaser must either (1) be without notice of the prior interest (notice statute), (2) be without notice of the prior interest and record first (race-notice statute), or (3) record first (race statute). In all jurisdictions, the prior interest holder may preserve the holder's original priority position by recording the interest immediately following its acquisition.

Illustration: MR executes a mortgage to ME–1 who records promptly. MR then executes a mortgage to ME–2. ME–2 cannot change the order of priority under any type of recording statute because ME–2 is on constructive notice of ME–1's prior interest and also has lost the race to record.

In this work it is assumed, unless otherwise indicated, that all mortgages and other interests were recorded immediately after their acquisition.

Mortgagees commonly turn to title insurance for assurance of lien priority. Mortgage loan arrangements frequently call for the acquisition of a lender's title insurance policy at the mortgagor's expense.

III. SELECTED ISSUES

Priority issues are inextricably entwined with the development of certain fundamental mortgage concepts. Thus, several priority problems are discussed in earlier chapters. *See* Ch. 4, pp. 76–85 (future advances and dragnet clause), Ch. 5, pp. 103–104 (after-acquired property clause), Ch. 6, pp. 121–122 (acquisition of mortgaged property by mortgagee), and Ch. 7, pp. 147–155 (conflicting and fractional assignments). Additional selected priority matters are presented here.

A. PURCHASE MONEY MORTGAGE

1. Distinguishing Features

A purchase money mortgage is a mortgage taken by the seller of real estate as security for part of the purchase price or by a third party lender as security for purchase funds advanced. *See* Ch. 3, pp. 52–53 (describing purchase money mortgage). In either situation, purchase money mortgage status is available only when the deed and the mortgage are components of a single transaction.

Illustration: MR desires to purchase certain land for sale in another part of the state. MR does not have sufficient cash on hand to do so. Thus, MR asks ME for a $20,000 loan. ME advances MR $20,000 to purchase the land. MR gives ME a $20,000 promissory note and agrees to secure the note with a mortgage on the property when MR acquires it. Later that day MR travels to the land and makes an offer to purchase it. After three days of protracted negotiations the transaction is completed, and MR receives a deed to the property. MR returns home. On the second day following MR's return, MR executes a mortgage on the property to ME. This is a purchase money mortgage. As long as the mortgage is an inseparable aspect of the acquisition of the mortgaged property, it need not be executed at the same time as the deed. *See* Stewart v. Smith, 30 N.W. 430 (Minn.1886).

2. Preferred Priority Position

A purchase money mortgage has priority over any pre-mortgage interest attaching to the realty via the purchaser-mortgagor. Underlying this principle is the equitable theory that when the mortgagor receives the property, it is already encumbered with a lien in favor of the purchase money mortgagee whose willingness to extend credit or advance funds made the acquisition possible. Accordingly, a purchase money mortgage takes precedence over judgment liens against the mortgagor, liens arising from after-acquired property clauses in other mortgages executed by the mortgagor, and claims against the mortgagor for dower or homestead.

Illustration: JL obtains a judgment against MR and receives a judgment lien on all real estate owned by MR. Later MR borrows money from ME to purchase a parcel of land. MR executes a mortgage on the land to ME to secure repayment of the loan. Under the purchase money mortgage rule, ME's mortgage lien has priority over JL's judgment lien.

The priority of a lien or other interest existing on the property at the time of its acquisition by the mortgagor is not affected by the purchase money mortgage rule. The rule only postpones the priority of liens and claims that attach to the realty via the purchaser-mortgagor.

Illustration: O owns a parcel of land. JL obtains a judgment against O and receives a judgment lien on all real estate owned by O, including the land in question. O then conveys the land to MR. The judgment lien is not discharged. MR pays O with funds borrowed from ME and executes a mortgage on the land to ME to secure repayment of the loan. Although ME's mortgage qualifies as a purchase money mortgage, it does not take precedence over JL's prior judgment lien on the land.

B.   SUBORDINATION AGREEMENTS

Established priorities may be altered by agreement. Such an agreement is called a subordination because it involves a senior interest holder voluntarily subordinating its rights to those of a junior interest holder. Three common subordination situations are treated here.

1.   Subordination of Purchase Money Mortgage to Construction Loan Mortgage

a.   *Background*

Subordination agreements are frequently employed as part of the real estate development process. Developers, of course, need raw land upon which to construct shopping centers, apartment houses, office buildings, subdivisions, and other projects. Because developers are typically unable to purchase land outright and because institutional lenders commonly are reluctant to make land acquisition loans, sellers often finance the sale themselves. This form of financing is not difficult to implement. The seller agrees to convey the land to the developer in exchange for a small down payment and a note for the balance of the purchase price secured by a purchase money mortgage on the land. The developer then obtains financing for the actual development. Construction lenders, however, normally demand a first lien on the property as security. In order for the planned development to occur, the seller, therefore, must subordinate the purchase money mortgage to the construction loan mortgage. The seller is usually willing to take this risk on the expectation that the development will enhance the property's value to the extent that the seller will be in a better security position as a second mortgagee of improved land than as a first mortgagee of unimproved land. Moreover, the seller ordinarily is able to demand a higher than normal purchase price for the property as compensation for agreeing to the subordination.

b. *Subordination Agreement in General*

The subordination is normally part of the original agreement between the seller and the developer and is covered in either the real estate contract, the purchase money mortgage, or a separate document. An advance subordination agreement may take either of two forms: (1) an agreement that subordination occurs automatically when the construction loan mortgage is executed or (2) an agreement to execute a formal subordination upon request once the construction loan is obtained.

c. *Describing Construction Loan*

The subordination agreement must contain an adequate description of the construction loan. If the subordination agreement does not, courts refuse to enforce the agreement on the ground it is impossible to tell what has been promised.

The question of whether the description of the construction loan is so indefinite as to render the subordination contract unenforceable is frequently difficult to resolve. Although courts generally agree that the maximum amount of the construction loan must be stated and fairly often also require that an interest rate cap be specified, they disagree as to whether the maturity, use of proceeds, or other loan details must be spelled out. Furthermore, some courts may enforce a less detailed subordination agreement when the missing terms are left for determination to an institutional construction lender. This approach is based on the rationale that institutional lenders are bound by regulation, custom, and usage to impose reasonable loan terms.

In California, the indefinite description issue is further complicated by a court decision requiring all subordination agreements to be just and reasonable with respect to the seller-purchase money mortgagee. Handy v. Gordon, 55 Cal.Rptr. 769 (Cal.1967). What this "fairness" doctrine demands regarding precision in describing the construction loan remains an open question.

d. Obtaining Construction Loan Described

If the developer obtains a construction loan that varies materially from the loan described in the subordination agreement, subordination does not occur.

e. Diversion of Construction Loan Funds

Priority problems may arise even after the specified construction loan is obtained. Occasionally, a mortgagor-developer diverts loan proceeds from the project with the result that the property is not sufficiently enhanced in value to adequately secure the subordinated purchase money mortgage loan. In such case, the seller-purchase money mortgagee is likely to claim that the subordination agreement has been breached and that the original lien priority has been restored. When this issue first arose, the courts typically held that, absent an agreement to the contrary, a construction loan mortgagee acting in good faith has no duty to monitor the application of construction funds. The construction lender, therefore, retains the lien priority granted to it in the subordination agreement unless it advances money to the developer in bad faith.

This principle survives, but its significance has been eroded by several developments. First, sellers-purchase money mortgagees commonly condition subordination upon actual use of the construction loan funds for construction purposes. Second, a similar condition may be implied in certain cases.

See Middlebrook–Anderson Co. v. Southwest Savings and Loan Association, 96 Cal.Rptr. 338 (Cal. App.1971). Third, some courts have concluded that construction lenders owe subordinated lienors a duty to exercise reasonable care in disbursing construction loan funds.

When subordination is expressly or impliedly conditioned upon the proper application of loan proceeds and funds are diverted, the seller-purchase money mortgagee is entitled to relief. The purchase money mortgage ordinarily should be restored to priority over the construction loan mortgage to the extent of the diverted funds. Thus, lien priority generally should be established as follows: (1) construction lender for funds properly applied to the project, (2) seller-purchase money mortgagee for the full amount of the purchase money mortgage, and (3) construction lender for diverted funds. There is, however, authority that the seller-purchase money mortgagee should be reinstated to first lien priority when the construction lender breaches an express condition to subordination.

f. *Optional Advance Risk*

Even if all funds are used for construction, the construction lender may lose priority to the subordinated purchase money mortgage for advances made ahead of schedule or after default on the theory such advances are optional, not obligatory. *See* Ch. 4, pp. 82–84 (considering construction lender's dilemma).

2. Subordination of Lease to Mortgage and Vice Versa

A mortgagee may desire to enhance its security position by switching priorities with a lessee of the mortgaged property. Reversal of priorities may occur in either direction. If a lease unattractive to the mortgagee has original priority, the mortgagee might demand subordination of the lease to the mortgage as a condition of making the mortgage loan. The subordination enables the mortgagee to terminate the lease if the mortgagee takes possession after default or forecloses. If a lease attractive to the mortgagee is originally junior to the mortgage, the mortgagee might subordinate the mortgage to the lease in order to collect rents from the lessee on default and preserve the lease beyond foreclosure. *See* Ch. 8, pp. 172–174 (analyzing problem of leases existing at default).

3. Subordination of Fee to Leasehold Mortgage

Leasehold mortgagees frequently require the owner of the leased property to submit the fee simple to the mortgage lien. Although this arrangement is commonly termed subordination of the fee, it obviously does not involve switching lien priorities. *See* Ch. 3, pp. 69–71 (discussing leasehold mortgage).

C. FIXTURES

A mortgage is a lien on all fixtures on the mortgaged property. *See* Ch. 5, pp. 105–106 (treating mortgage coverage of fixtures). These fixtures also may be subject to the lien of a security interest that attached to them before they became fixtures. In that event, a contest results between the mortgagee and the holder of the security interest regarding the priority of their respective liens. Section 9–334 of the Uniform Commercial Code (UCC) is designed to resolve this priority issue. Following is a summary of its most significant provisions.

As a general rule of UCC § 9–334, priority between the holder of a security interest in fixtures and the mortgagee goes to the first one to properly file in the public records. A purchase money security interest filed before or within twenty days after items of personal property become fixtures, however, takes priority over existing nonconstruction loan mortgages on the theory that the party who supplies the money used to acquire the fixtures should be favored. But, because a construction lender provides funds for the entire improvement and expects all parts thereof to serve as collateral for its loan, existing construction loan mortgages take priority over purchase money security interests in items of personal property that become fixtures during construction. Finally, with regard to the recordation process, the UCC requires that fixture financing statements be filed and indexed in local real estate records so a person conducting a title search can discover them. *See* UCC §§ 9–501(a), 9–519(d).

D. MECHANICS' LIEN STATUTES

1. General

Mechanics' lien statutes accord parties supplying services, labor, or materials to a construction project a lien on the realty for payment due. These universally enacted measures vary greatly among the states with regard to parties protected, lien amount, lien priority, and other matters. Only amount, priority, and constitutional issues are treated here.

2. Amount

Mechanics' lien statutes generally take one of two markedly different approaches regarding the amount that a lien claimant may recover. Some states, following the New York system, view the rights of mechanics' lienors as derived from the general construction contract and thus limit recovery to the balance due on the contract at the date the lien is filed. Other jurisdictions, adopting the Pennsylvania system, give mechanics' lien claimants direct rights and therefore permit recovery for the full value of their labor, goods, or services.

3. Priority

Priority problems frequently arise between mechanics' lienors and mortgagees, particularly construction mortgage lenders. In order to resolve these issues, it is necessary to ascertain the priority accorded mechanics' liens under local statutes. The statutes are far from uniform on this subject.

a. *Relation Back to Commencement of Construction*

In numerous states, a mechanics' lienor's priority relates back to when construction began. Under this approach, the construction lender can protect its mortgage lien against all mechanics' lienors by recording the construction loan mortgage before construction commences. But, if the lender fails to do so, it loses priority to all mechanics' lienors, not just those who did work before the mortgage was recorded.

> *Illustration*: MR decides to construct a building on MR's property, so MR hires X to clear the land and do the necessary excavation work. X completes the job and is paid by MR. Six weeks later, MR obtains a construction mortgage loan from ME who promptly records the mortgage. After the mortgage is recorded, Y does work on the building. Y is not paid. Y, therefore, files a mechanics' lien. Y's lien relates back to when X performed the initial construction work on the project and thereby takes priority over ME's mortgage.

Even if the construction loan mortgage is recorded before work begins, controversy may develop as to the priority of future advances made by a construction lender over an intervening mechanics' lien. This issue usually arises when a mechanics' lienor contends that all construction advances made after the attachment of its mechanics' lien are optional, not obligatory, and thereby lose priority to its encumbrance. *See* Ch. 4, pp. 82–84 (considering construction lender's dilemma).

b. Other Approaches

The remaining states take a wide variety of approaches to the mechanics' lien priority issue. Certain jurisdictions grant lien priority from the date the mechanics' lienor actually began work or supplied materials. In some states, the lien receives priority as of the day the lien claimant files. Other jurisdictions base lien priority on additional considerations, such as the time the general construction contract was entered.

4. Constitutionality of Mechanics' Lien Statutes

Mechanics' lien statutes generally authorize mechanics and materialmen to perfect their liens without judicial involvement and sometimes without prior notice to the property owner. This procedure has been attacked in several jurisdictions as a denial of the landowner's Fourteenth Amendment due process rights.

Most courts faced with this issue have upheld the mechanics' lien statute in question on the theory that a mechanics' lien does not constitute a taking of property within the meaning of the Fourteenth Amendment. These courts reason that the attachment of the lien does not deprive the owner of possession, use, or enjoyment of the land and any impairment of the owner's ability to sell or encumber the property is merely a de minimis taking that does not trigger the application of procedural due process safeguards. A few courts, however, have concluded that a mechanics' lien affects a Fourteenth Amendment property interest by impairing the property owner's ability to alienate the land and also by reducing the value of the owner's equity. Some of these courts further held that local statutory procedures for perfecting mechanics' liens were constitutionally defective on due process grounds.

5. Other Protection for Mechanics and Materialmen

It is noted earlier in this section that in most states a prudent construction lender may secure priority over a mechanics' lienor by recording the construction loan mortgage before construction commences. Hence, if the project fails and the mortgagee forecloses, mechanics' lienors usually receive nothing from the foreclosure sale. To correct this inequity, some states have given mechanics and materialmen lien rights in addition to those they receive under the traditional mechanics' lien statute.

a. *Stop Notice Statutes*

In some jurisdictions, parties who have supplied services, labor, or materials to a construction project may obtain a statutory lien on construction loan money not yet disbursed by the lender. Legislation of this type is known as a stop notice statute. These statutes differ in various respects. As a general proposition, a stop notice statute permits an unpaid mechanic or materialman to file a notice of claim with the lender who then must stop advancing funds for construction or, at least, withhold funds to cover the claim.

b. Equitable Liens

A number of courts have used the equitable lien concept to fashion a remedy for mechanics and materialman similar to that available under stop notice statutes. Under the equitable lien approach, an unpaid lien claimant may reach undisbursed construction loan funds if the claimant can show special equities or establish that the lender has been unjustly enriched.

E. TAX LIENS

1. State and Local Real Estate Tax Liens

Statutes in most states impose a lien on real estate to secure the payment of taxes or assessments levied on the land. Usually these real estate tax and assessment liens are allowed to leapfrog existing encumbrances to the first lien priority position. In order to minimize the risk of losing priority to subsequent tax liens, mortgagees commonly require the mortgagor to escrow funds for the payment of real property taxes. *See* Ch. 4, pp. 96–98 (discussing escrow accounts).

2. Federal Income Tax Liens

The federal government may obtain a lien against the real property of a delinquent income taxpayer.

Unlike state and local real estate tax liens, a federal tax lien does not receive priority over existing encumbrances. It also is not valid against subsequent mortgages until notice of its existence is filed in the public land records. Even a properly filed federal tax lien loses priority to certain interests that arise subsequent to its filing, such as real estate tax liens and certain mechanics' liens. *See* 26 U.S.C.A. §§ 6321–6323. Numerous other priority issues exist under federal tax lien law, but they are beyond the scope of this work.

F.   LIS PENDENS

Under the common law doctrine of lis pendens, the pendency of a suit concerning title to or possession of land imparts constructive notice to the world of the claims of the litigants. One who acquires an interest in real estate involved in litigation, therefore, takes subject to the judgment of the court. Because it is often difficult to discover the existence of pending litigation, statutes in most states limit the application of the lis pendens doctrine by requiring that a separate notice of the suit be filed.

Illustration: O conveys land to GE who records. O initiates suit to have the deed set aside and records a lis pendens notice as required by state law. GE executes a mortgage on the land to ME. The court then renders judgment in favor of O and sets aside the deed. Because ME was on lis pendens notice of O's interest, O takes the property free from ME's mortgage. In those states that continue to follow the common law lis pendens doctrine, O would take free from the mortgage even if O had failed to file separate notice of the suit.

G. MARSHALING

The equitable doctrine of marshaling assets does not deal so much with determining the priority of interests in the mortgaged property as with equitably preserving the value of each interest once priority has been established. The doctrine has two main facets: the two funds rule and the sale in inverse order of alienation rule. These principles of marshaling overlap somewhat; both may be applicable in certain situations. Matters are complicated further by conflict over what particular circumstances call for the application of each rule.

1. Two Funds Rule

The two funds rule is the most familiar principle of marshaling. It provides that when a senior mortgagee has a claim against two funds and a junior mortgagee has a claim against only one of them, the senior mortgagee must enforce its claim so as to best preserve the value of the junior mortgagee's security. Although the senior mortgagee may proceed at law against either or both funds, equity requires it to seek satisfaction first from the fund the junior mortgagee cannot reach. Only when this fund is exhausted may the senior mortgagee proceed against the sole fund to which the junior mortgagee has access.

Illustration: MR owns two parcels of land, lot A worth $10,000 and lot B worth $4,000. MR borrows $12,000 from ME–1 and gives ME–1 a first mortgage on both lots. MR then borrows $5,000 from ME–2 and gives ME–2 a second mortgage on lot A. MR defaults on both mortgages. ME–1 forecloses on lot A only, and the foreclosure sale brings $10,000. ME–1 claims the entire amount as first lienor. Although ME–1's $12,000 mortgage was a first lien on lot A, under the two funds rule ME–1 receives foreclosure sale proceeds as if it had satisfied itself first out of lot B and then out of lot A. Under this principle, ME–1 receives $8,000 (the amount of its lien minus the value of lot B), and ME–2 is entitled to $2,000.

Illustration: Assume the same fact situation as in the immediately preceding illustration except that no default occurs and ME–1 releases its lien on lot B even though it actually knows of ME–2's second mortgage on lot A. Under the two funds rule, ME–1 retains a first lien on lot A for only $8,000 (the amount of the original lien minus the value of lot B), and ME–2 has a second lien for $5,000.

2.   Sale in Inverse Order of Alienation Rule

The doctrine of marshaling also applies when a large tract of mortgaged land is subdivided and sold in separate parcels to parties who pay the full purchase price for their lots without obtaining a partial release of the blanket mortgage. If the blanket mortgage was recorded, its lien follows each lot into the hands of the lot purchaser. (Payment of the full purchase price to the mortgagor does not discharge the mortgagee's lien.) Although the purchaser would not have consummated the deal if the purchaser had searched the title, the purchaser is not completely unprotected. Equity gives the purchaser the right to require that the land retained by the seller be sold at foreclosure before the purchaser's lot is sold. Because this concept favors purchasers in the order they acquired lots, it is called the sale in inverse order of alienation rule.

Illustration: MR owns a ten-acre tract subject to a recorded mortgage in favor of ME. MR subdivides the tract into ten one-acre lots and sells lots A and B successively to purchasers who each pay the full sale price for their respective lots. MR defaults on the blanket mortgage, and ME forecloses. Under the sale in inverse order of alienation rule, equity requires the court to direct the sheriff to sell first the land retained by MR, next lot B, and finally lot A. The sale process ends whenever the cumulative proceeds are sufficient to satisfy the mortgage debt.

The sale in inverse order of alienation rule is limited in several respects. First, the rule is inapplicable when a purchaser pays a reduced purchase price for taking the property subject to the mortgage. Second, most purchasers making full payment search the records and demand a partial release of the mortgage. Third, the mortgagee may avoid application of the rule by placing an anti-marshaling clause in the mortgage.

3.   Anti–Marshaling Clause

Courts generally will not apply marshaling in either of its forms in the face of a contrary agreement. Mortgagees, therefore, often insist on a mortgage provision giving them the right to release or foreclose and sell parcels of the mortgaged property free from any requirement to marshal assets.

CHAPTER 10

FORECLOSURE

The evolution of the foreclosure concept is traced in Chapter 1. This chapter is designed to promote understanding of the procedure as it presently exists.

I. AVAILABILITY AND PURPOSE

Upon default, the mortgagee may have the mortgaged property sold to satisfy the unpaid mortgage debt. *See* Ch. 1, pp. 6–8 (discussing development of foreclosure by sale). Although this process is customarily referred to as mortgage foreclosure, it is really the mortgagor's equity of redemption that is foreclosed.

The foreclosure process generally may be commenced by the mortgagee anytime after default. *See* Ch. 8, pp. 162–169 (discussing default and acceleration). *But see* p. 227 (noting state legislation enacted in response to 2007–2008 foreclosure escalation). Its purpose is to cut off the mortgagor's equity of redemption and the rights of all parties who acquired interests in the land after the mortgage was executed, so that whoever purchases the property at foreclosure receives title as it existed in the hands of the mortgagor immediately before the mortgage attached. An important corollary of this principle is that interests acquired by third parties prior to the execution of the mortgage survive foreclosure. As a result, the mortgagee obtains the full benefit of the security for which it bargained, but no more.

II. STATUTE OF LIMITATIONS

In most states, the mortgagee must foreclose within a certain statutory period after maturity of the mortgage. Because needless controversy arises when the statute of limitations on the mortgage and the underlying debt differ, several jurisdictions have enacted statutes that bar the enforcement of both simultaneously. *See*, Ch. 4, p. 101 (analyzing problem presented when statute of limitations runs on debt, but not on mortgage).

III. FEDERAL LEGISLATION AFFECTING FORECLOSURE

A. MORTGAGOR IN BANKRUPTCY

Following is a discussion of two significant ways that proceedings under the federal Bankruptcy Code may intrude on the foreclosure process. Various other aspects of bankruptcy law also may affect foreclosure.

1. Automatic Stay of Foreclosure Proceedings

The mortgagor's bankruptcy may significantly alter the mortgagee's right to foreclose. The filing of any form of bankruptcy petition automatically stays foreclosure proceedings against the mortgagor. 11 U.S.C.A. § 362(a). The Department of Housing and Urban Development, however, receives a limited exception from this automatic stay rule; it may still foreclose certain multi-living-unit mortgages it holds. 11 U.S.C.A. § 362(b)(8). Moreover, the automatic stay principle is restricted in certain ways to deter its misuse via repetitive petitions. 11 U.S.C.A. § 362(c)(3)-(4).

The bankruptcy court may grant the mortgagee relief from the automatic stay in certain situations. Relief may be granted (1) "for cause, including the lack of adequate protection" of the mortgagee's interest; (2) when the mortgagor does not have any equity in the mortgaged property, and the "property is not necessary to an effective reorganization;" (3) when provisions covering "single asset real estate" are met; or (4) when "the petition was part of a scheme to delay, hinder, and defraud creditors that involved either" a transfer of the mortgaged realty without the mortgagee's consent or a court's approval, or "multiple bankruptcy filings affecting such real property." 11 U.S.C.A. § 362(d).

2. Nullification of Prior Foreclosure Sale

Problems may arise even when the mortgagor enters bankruptcy after the foreclosure process has been completed. A bankruptcy trustee may set aside a prior foreclosure sale as a fraudulent transfer if the sale was held within two years of the bankruptcy petition filing at a time the mortgagor was insolvent, and the sale price did not constitute "reasonably equivalent value." 11 U.S.C.A. § 548. For many years, disagreement existed regarding how to determine "reasonably equivalent value." Ultimately the issue reached the Supreme Court where the justices concluded that the proceeds produced by a properly conducted state foreclosure sale satisfy the "reasonably equivalent value" standard. *See* BFP v. Resolution Trust Corp., 511 U.S. 531 (1994).

Although courts are divided on the issue, a bankruptcy trustee may seek to avoid a prior foreclosure sale as a preference when a number of conditions are met. In general terms, a voidable preference may be found when the mortgagee purchases at a foreclosure sale conducted within ninety days of the bankruptcy petition filing at a time the mortgagor was insolvent, and the mortgagee thereby received more value than it would have obtained in a straight bankruptcy liquidation. 11 U.S.C.A. § 547(b).

B. MORTGAGOR IN MILITARY SERVICE

The Servicemembers Civil Relief Act, 50 U.S.C.A. App. § 501 *et seq.*, grants special protection to mortgagors on active duty in the armed forces. Thus, the Act, particularly its default judgment and stay portions, should be consulted whenever a servicemember-mortgagor faces foreclosure.

IV. FORECLOSURE BY JUDICIAL SALE

Foreclosure by judicially approved sale constitutes the backbone of our system of mortgage foreclosure. *See* Ch. 1, pp. 6–8 (discussing development of foreclosure by sale). Such a proceeding is available in all states and the required method of foreclosure in a number of jurisdictions. Although court supervised foreclosure is the best way to ascertain the rights of the parties involved and thereby to produce the most marketable title, it is often a complex, protracted, and expensive procedure. Legal difficulties inherent in this process are analyzed in this section.

A. PARTIES DEFENDANT

A foreclosure decree affects only those persons before the court. Naming parties defendant, therefore, is a critical step in the foreclosure process.

1. Necessary/Proper Parties

Parties defendant can be placed into two general categories—necessary parties and proper parties. A necessary party defendant to a foreclosure suit is anyone who must be joined in order to accomplish the objective of foreclosure which, as previously noted, is to sell the mortgagor's interest in the property as it existed immediately before the execution of the mortgage. Thus, the mortgagor and all persons who acquired interests in the property after the execution of the mortgage are necessary parties and may be joined without their consent. The interests of necessary parties omitted from the suit survive foreclosure.

   Illustration: MR executes a first mortgage to ME–1. MR then executes a second mortgage to ME–2, leases a part of the mortgaged land to L, and grants an easement over another part to X. MR defaults on the first mortgage, and ME–1 commences foreclosure proceedings. MR, ME–2, L, and X are all necessary parties defendant because their interests must be extinguished if the foreclosure sale purchaser is to receive MR's interest as it existed immediately before the first mortgage was executed.

A proper party defendant to a foreclosure suit is one whose joinder is desirable, but not essential to achieve the purpose of foreclosure. Senior mortgagees and those who hold no interest in the property, but are personally liable on the debt are proper parties. Although an individual personally liable on the debt can be involuntarily joined, a senior mortgagee generally cannot be joined without its consent.

2.   Intentional Omission of Junior Lessees

When a junior lease is particularly favorable to the lessor, it is to the mortgagee's advantage to keep the lease alive through foreclosure and thereby enhance the sale value of its security. Because the rights of a junior interest holder not made a party defendant survive foreclosure, it would appear that a mortgagee could preserve a valuable junior lease by intentionally omitting the lessee from the foreclosure suit. Certain jurisdictions allow the mort-gagee to keep a junior lease alive in this fashion. Elsewhere, however, foreclosure extinguishes an intentionally omitted junior lease, at least when the lessee does not want to preserve it. This approach may be justified on the ground that joinder requirements are for the protection of junior interest holders, not the mortgagee.

In view of the uncertainty that exists with regard to preserving intentionally omitted junior leases, a mortgagee sometimes will subordinate the mortgage to a valuable junior lease to insure that the lease will survive foreclosure. *See* Ch. 8, pp. 172–174 (considering problem of junior leases existing at default); Ch. 9, p. 195 (discussing subordination of mortgage to lease).

3. Lis Pendens

Under the doctrine of lis pendens, parties who acquire an interest in the mortgaged property with notice of the foreclosure proceedings are bound by the foreclosure decree just as if they had been named parties defendant. *See* Ch. 9, pp. 202–203 (analyzing doctrine of lis pendens).

B.   SALE PROCEDURES

The judicial foreclosure sale procedure is governed by statutory law that varies from state to state. These statutes normally call for a public sale conducted by the sheriff or a court appointed official.

C. CONFIRMATION/ADEQUACY OF SALE PRICE

Foreclosure by judicial sale is not final until the sale is confirmed by the court. Absent fraud or chilled bidding, inadequacy of the foreclosure sale price is generally not a ground upon which courts withhold confirmation. Statutes in some states require that the sale price be a specified fraction of the appraised value of the property, e.g., two-thirds, but in certain of these jurisdictions, mortgagors commonly waive appraisal.

D. PURCHASER

1. Purchaser's Title

The purchaser at a judicial foreclosure sale receives title to the property as it existed in the hands of the mortgagor immediately before the execution of the mortgage. Although the rights of the mortgagor, the mortgagee, and junior interest holders named parties defendant are extinguished, the rights of individuals who acquired interests prior to the execution of the mortgage survive foreclosure.

Illustration: MR grants an easement over MR's land to X. MR then executes a first mortgage to ME–1, a second mortgage to ME–2, a third mortgage to ME–3, and a lease of part of the property to L. ME–2 forecloses, naming all necessary parties in the suit. *See* pp. 211–212 (discussing necessary/proper parties). P acquires title at the foreclosure sale. Although the interests of MR, ME–2,

ME–3, and L end at foreclosure, P takes the property subject to the interests of X and ME–1.

In addition, because the foreclosure sale proceeds are used to satisfy the mortgage debt, the purchaser is subrogated to the rights of the mortgagee. *See* Ch. 7, pp. 155–160 (analyzing subrogation—assignment by operation of law). This concept is important in determining the purchaser's position vis-à-vis a junior lienor omitted from the original foreclosure proceeding.

2. Purchaser Versus Omitted Junior Lienor

When a junior lienor is not named as a party defendant, the junior lien survives foreclosure. The omitted junior lienor still may either foreclose its junior lien or redeem the senior mortgage. *See* Ch. 8, pp. 180–181 (analyzing redemption by junior interest holder). The purchaser at the foreclosure sale, however, may eliminate the omitted junior lien by using any one of three methods—redemption, reforeclosure, or possibly strict foreclosure. As successor to the mortgagor's right of equity of redemption, the purchaser may extinguish the omitted junior lien by paying it off. *See* Ch. 8, p. 180 (discussing redemption by mortgagor or mortgagor's successor). The purchaser also is subrogated to the mortgagee's right to foreclose. The purchaser, therefore, may eliminate the omitted junior lien by reforeclosing the mortgage with the junior lienor now included or, in certain jurisdictions, by strictly foreclosing the rights of the junior lienor.

3. Purchase by Mortgagee

The mortgagee may purchase the mortgaged property at the foreclosure sale. Because the mortgagee is entitled to receive as much of the sale proceeds as is necessary to satisfy the mortgage debt, the mortgagee may bid up to that amount without having to produce any cash. As a consequence, the mortgagee frequently is the highest bidder at the foreclosure sale.

4. Purchase by Mortgagor

If the mortgagor or the mortgagor's agent purchases at the foreclosure sale, unpaid junior liens typically survive on the theory that the purchase was really payment of the senior lien. This is, of course, an exception to the rule that all properly joined junior interests are cut off by foreclosure.

E. DISTRIBUTION OF PROCEEDS

The proceeds of the foreclosure sale are distributed in the following order: (1) payment of foreclosure expenses, (2) discharge of the mortgage debt, and (3) satisfaction of junior liens, as well as other junior interests, in the order of their priority. Any excess belongs to the current owner of the property, who in most cases is the mortgagor.

F. DEFICIENCY JUDGMENT

1. General

If the foreclosure sale proceeds are insufficient to satisfy the underlying debt, the mortgagee generally

may obtain a deficiency judgment against the mortgagor and anyone else personally liable on the debt.

Illustration: MR executes a $10,000 promissory
note and a mortgage to ME. MR conveys the
property to GE who assumes and agrees to pay
the mortgage debt. GE defaults, and ME forecloses. The foreclosure sale produces $8,000 after
expenses. ME receives the $8,000 and generally
may obtain a deficiency judgment for $2,000
against each MR and GE. Naturally, ME may
recover no more than $2,000 on these judgments.

2. Anti–Deficiency Legislation

Depression era legislation still restricts the recovery of deficiency judgments in a number of jurisdictions. One statutory approach is to prohibit deficiency judgments in certain situations, such as in
the case of purchase money mortgages or when
foreclosure is by power of sale. Another approach is
to limit deficiency judgments to the amount by
which the debt exceeds the fair market value of the
property. Waiver of the protection provided by anti-
deficiency legislation is generally considered ineffective as against public policy.

V. FORECLOSURE BY POWER OF SALE

Foreclosure by out-of-court sale is recognized in a
substantial majority of states. *See* Ch. 1, pp. 6–8
(discussing development of foreclosure by sale).
This method of foreclosure usually is termed foreclosure by power of sale because it is based on a

mortgage provision authorizing sale of the property without court supervision. Although foreclosure by power of sale represents a relatively expedient and inexpensive means of foreclosure, it is prohibited in a number of jurisdictions and where permitted, it exists as an alternative to foreclosure by judicial sale. See Ch. 12, pp. 237–238, 240–243 (treating reform measures employing out-of-court foreclosure).

A. COMPARISON TO JUDICIAL SALE

Foreclosure by power of sale serves generally the same purpose and produces essentially the same result as foreclosure by judicial sale. However, some significant differences exist.

1. Form of Security Device

Because the deed of trust is designed to be enforced by an out-of-court sale conducted by the trustee, it is a popular financing device in most states where foreclosure by power of sale is permitted. *See* Ch. 1, pp. 7–8 & Ch. 3, pp. 54–55 (discussing deed of trust). A standard mortgage, of course, may be drafted to include a power of sale provision.

2. Sale Procedures

The procedure for foreclosure by power of sale generally is regulated by statute. These statutes normally provide for a public sale conducted only after proper notice. Typically, notice by advertisement in a local newspaper for a prescribed period is required. In certain jurisdictions, additional notice must be given to the mortgagor by personal service or mail. Junior interest holders usually are not entitled to such added notice.

3. Purchaser's Title

The purchaser at a power of sale foreclosure receives the same rights as a purchaser at a judicial foreclosure. Nonetheless, the title of the purchaser at a power of sale foreclosure generally is less secure because the sale has not been confirmed by a court and is, therefore, more likely to be the subject of future litigation.

4. Purchase by Lender

The form of the financing device authorizing foreclosure by power of sale determines whether the lender may bid at the sale. If a mortgage with a power of sale provision is involved, the mortgagee has a duty to conduct the sale in an impartial manner. Thus, the mortgagee may not purchase the property unless it has contractual or statutory permission to do so. If a deed of trust is used, the lender may freely bid because the trustee conducts the sale.

5. Deficiency or Surplus

Foreclosure by power of sale is conducted outside the judicial system. Consequently, the mortgagee may need to initiate a legal proceeding when either a deficiency or a surplus results. If the proceeds are insufficient to satisfy the mortgage debt, the mortgagee must bring suit to recover a deficiency judgment against a party personally liable on the underlying obligation. As discussed earlier in this chapter, deficiency judgments are subject to legislative prohibition or limitation in certain jurisdictions. *See* p. 217 (discussing anti-deficiency legislation). If the proceeds exceed the amount of the mortgage debt, the mortgagee may file an interpleader action to guard against liability for paying the surplus to the wrong parties.

6. Judicial Review

Although the courts do not oversee foreclosure by power of sale, the process is always subject to later judicial scrutiny. This possibility reduces the value of the property to prospective purchasers and may cause the mortgagee to forego foreclosure by power of sale in favor of foreclosure by judicial sale.

B.   CONSTITUTIONAL ISSUES

Foreclosure by power of sale has come under constitutional attack on the ground that the notice and hearing procedures used in the typical power of sale foreclosure do not meet the procedural due process requirements of the Fifth and Fourteenth Amendments. This attack really involves several issues.

1. Governmental Action

The Fifth and Fourteenth Amendments limit governmental action, not private activity. The first issue, therefore, is whether a power of sale foreclosure involves significant federal or state action.

The federal action question usually arises when the foreclosing mortgagee is connected to the federal government in some way. The few courts that have considered the question have tended to find federal action if the mortgagee is a branch of the federal government such as the Department of Veterans Affairs, but not if it is a private entity closely related to the federal government such as Fannie Mae (previously the Federal National Mortgage Association or FNMA) and Freddie Mac (previously the Federal Home Loan Mortgage Corporation or FHLMC). Although there is some authority that the Government National Mortgage Association (GNMA or popularly Ginnie Mae) is not a federal instrumentality bound by due process restrictions, such a hybrid organization is difficult to categorize. Thus, the federal action question remains partly unresolved.

The state action question is relatively well settled. The prevailing view is that power of sale foreclosure does not involve state action. Courts generally conclude that this method of foreclosure is established by private contract even though it may be recognized and regulated by state statute. *See* Apao v. Bank of New York, 324 F.3d 1091 (9th Cir.2003). Unsuccessful arguments for state action have been based on encouragement, enforcement, and participation theories.

2. Notice and Hearing

In those instances in which foreclosure by power of sale is considered to involve governmental action, procedural due process mandates that the mortgagor and other interested parties receive sufficient notice of the foreclosure and a presale opportunity to be heard. In order to determine whether these requirements have been met, it is necessary to examine the mortgage documents in question and the applicable local statutes. Power of sale foreclosure procedures rarely satisfy due process standards. Notice published in a newspaper often is inadequate. Moreover, an opportunity for a presale hearing normally is not provided.

3. Waiver

Even assuming that the requisite governmental action is present and that the local procedure violates either the Fifth Amendment or the Fourteenth Amendment, a power of sale foreclosure still may be conducted if the mortgagor knowingly and voluntarily waives the mortgagor's procedural due process rights. The validity of individual waivers, of course, only can be determined on a case-by-case basis.

VI. STRICT FORECLOSURE

Strict foreclosure was the method originally used to extinguish the mortgagor's equity of redemption. After default, an equity court would establish a time period within which the mortgagor was required to pay the debt or lose the mortgaged land to the mortgagee. This means of foreclosure generally was not accepted in this country. *See* Ch. 1, p. 6

(discussing historical development of strict foreclosure). Today, strict foreclosure is available as a principal method of foreclosure in only a handful of states. In several other jurisdictions, however, its use is authorized against necessary parties omitted from a prior judicial foreclosure suit. *See* p. 215 (analyzing situations involving purchaser versus omitted junior lienors).

Statutes in a few northeastern states provide for a special form of strict foreclosure that is accomplished by entry plus possession for a specified time period which ranges between one and three years. The effect is the same as the traditional form of strict foreclosure; the mortgagor's equity of redemption is extinguished without a foreclosure sale of any kind.

VII. STATUTORY REDEMPTION
A. AVAILABILITY

Although the equity of redemption expires at foreclosure, statutes in approximately one-half of the states establish a right to redeem the mortgaged property *after* the foreclosure sale. *See* Ch. 1, p. 8 (discussing statutory redemption). The primary goal of statutory redemption is to protect the mortgagor, as well as junior lienors, from sale of the property at a price far below its value. An additional objective of these statutes is to give the mortgagor more time to obtain the funds necessary to retain the land. Statutory redemption laws vary considerably, but each establishes a time frame, such as one year, within which redemption must be accomplished. In certain jurisdictions, the local statutory redemption scheme is inapplicable to power of sale foreclosure.

As a general rule, the mortgagor may retain possession of the mortgaged real estate during the statutory redemption period. If redemption is not accomplished by the end of that period, the purchaser at the foreclosure sale receives title to and possession of the property.

B.   PARTIES WHO MAY REDEEM

The mortgagor, the mortgagor's successors, and any junior lienor joined in the foreclosure may exercise a right of redemption under most statutes. The mortgagor and the mortgagor's successors frequently receive an exclusive right to redeem for a specified period. After the mortgagor's redemption period has elapsed, junior lienors usually have the right to redeem in the order of their priority. Certain states have adopted other procedures for exercising statutory redemption rights.

C.   AMOUNT REQUIRED
FOR REDEMPTION

The amount required for statutory redemption is generally the foreclosure sale price together with interest as specified in the statute.

D.   RESULT OF REDEMPTION

1.   By Mortgagor or Mortgagor's Successor

Statutory redemption by the mortgagor or the mortgagor's successor annuls the foreclosure sale and restores title to the redeemer. Authorities differ, however, as to whether unsatisfied pre-existing junior liens are revived.

2.   By Junior Lienor

When a junior lienor redeems, the junior lienor generally receives the rights of the foreclosure sale purchaser. Other junior lien holders usually may redeem from the original redeemer.

E.   WAIVER

States are divided on the question of waiver of the statutory right of redemption. Some states prohibit waiver. At the opposite end of the spectrum, certain jurisdictions allow mortgagors to waive their statutory redemption rights by mortgage provision. Other states permit waiver only in limited situations, such as when the mortgagor is a corporation.

F.   COMPARISON TO EQUITY OF REDEMPTION

Statutory redemption often is confused with equity of redemption. *See* Ch. 1, pp. 4–5 & Ch. 8, pp. 179–182 (discussing equity of redemption). Although both methods of redemption are designed to protect the mortgagor, they differ significantly.

First, equity of redemption developed as a part of our common law and is available in all states. Statutory redemption is a legislative creation that exists in approximately one-half of the states. Second, the equity of redemption expires at foreclosure; statutory redemption schemes then become operative. An equity of redemption and a right of statutory redemption, therefore, cannot exist in the same party at the same time. Third, the equity of redemption generally is not extinguished at the end of any specific time. It lasts until terminated by foreclosure. Statutory redemption, however, exists within a precise time frame, running from foreclosure to the end of the period established by statute. Fourth, redemption in equity is from the mortgage. Redemption under statutory provision is from the foreclosure sale. Thus, the amount required for equitable redemption is the amount in default, usually the unpaid balance of the mortgage debt. The amount required for statutory redemption typically is based on the foreclosure sale price. Fifth, the right of equity of redemption may not be waived. Statutory redemption, however, may be waived by mortgage provision in some jurisdictions.

G. CRITICISM OF STATUTORY REDEMPTION

Statutory redemption has been roundly criticized on the ground that it does not really achieve its intended purpose—to produce realistic bids at the foreclosure sale. *See* United States v. Stadium Apartments, Inc., 425 F.2d 358 (9th Cir.1970).

Some critics have gone even further and suggested that statutory redemption is actually counterproductive. The fact that the purchaser must wait for a year or so before receiving the property may dampen bidding by outsiders and thereby depress the sale price. Moreover, this delay and its attendant risks may cause mortgagees to lend less or demand a higher rate of return in states that utilize a statutory redemption period to "protect" mortgagors.

VIII.   FORECLOSURE ESCALATION

Foreclosures escalated markedly in 2007–2008. Congress and state legislatures have taken various forms of action in response to this phenomenon, most notably the federal Housing and Economic Relief Act of 2008 (*see* Ch. 2, pp. 48–49) and the federal Emergency Economic Stabilization Act of 2008 (*see* Ch. 2, pp. 49–50). Moreover, legislators have weighed taking other steps. Regulatory bodies also have addressed the situation.

Delaying the commencement of foreclosure in some way is one approach that has received attention. Indeed, legislation that takes this tack has been enacted in certain states. If and how foreclosure procedures generally will be adjusted over the long run remains to be seen. *See* Ch. 12, pp. 236–243 (discussing reform measures).

CHAPTER 11

FINANCING COOPERATIVES AND CONDOMINIUMS

I. BACKGROUND

As the population of this country began to crowd our urban centers during the first half of the twentieth century, it became increasingly difficult for many people to realize the American dream of homeownership. Housing cooperatives and condominiums were developed in large part to meet the public's desire in this regard. Both offer individuals the opportunity to acquire a unit in a multi-unit building. Although cooperatives and condominiums are generally residential developments, either form of ownership may be used for a commercial project.

The cooperative and the condominium pose unique real estate finance problems. These issues are explored in this chapter, but first it is necessary to review the general legal principles underlying each form of development.

II. COOPERATIVES

A. COOPERATIVE CONCEPT

Cooperative apartments became popular in New York City during the early 1900s and soon spread to other major metropolitan areas. Title to the cooperative apartment building, as well as the land upon which it is located, ordinarily is held by a corporation. Stock in the corporation is allocated among the cooperative apartment units based upon their relative size or value, usually value. Each cooperative member purchases the stock assigned to a specific apartment and receives a long-term "proprietary" lease to that unit. Rent payable under the lease is the cooperative member's proportionate share of the expenses the corporation incurs in operating the cooperative. Expenses include costs for taxes, insurance, maintenance, management, and, as discussed below, mortgage debt service.

B.   FINANCING COOPERATIVES

1.   Construction or Acquisition Financing

In order to finance the purchase or construction of the cooperative building, the cooperative corporation places a blanket mortgage on the property. This general financing arrangement presents the individual cooperative members with certain financing problems.

2.   Loans on Units

Lending institutions may be reluctant or unable to take a cooperative member's stock and proprietary lease as security for a long-term loan. Although such loans are more readily available today than they were some time ago, cooperative apartment purchasers still may face considerable difficulty in obtaining adequate financing in many areas of the country. As a result, the purchaser of a cooperative apartment unit may be required to have enough ready cash to pay for the stock allocated to the unit or find a seller who is willing to recover the seller's equity in installments over a number of years.

3.   Default on Blanket Mortgage

The financial interdependence of the cooperative members is another source of concern. The existence of a blanket mortgage paid by rent receipts means that if some members fail to pay rent, the cooperative may not have sufficient funds to meet a mortgage loan installment. The entire membership is then faced with foreclosure unless they take action to cure the default. Although reserves and special assessments may be utilized to cover such a contingency, there is always the possibility that available funds will be inadequate and that all cooperative members will be at the mercy of the blanket mortgagee.

III.   CONDOMINIUMS

A.   CONDOMINIUM CONCEPT

Although cooperative apartment members are more than ordinary tenants, they do not hold title to their units. Condominium owners do. This idea of separate ownership of housing units in a multi-unit building originated long ago and was utilized throughout Europe in the Middle Ages.

Condominium development achieved prominence in the United States only relatively recently. Changes in economic, political, and social conditions precipitated dramatic condominium growth in this country since the early 1960s. The combination of a land shortage in populous regions, legislation in each state establishing guidelines for the creation of condominiums, and the possibility of insuring mortgages on individual condominium units caused condominium developments to spring up in such number that they now occupy a significant position in the overall housing picture. Commercial condominiums are also quite common. As might be expected, the cooperative dwindled in importance in the real estate marketplace as the condominium rose in popularity.

A condominium is created when a developer records a formal declaration that the developer submits certain real estate to the local condominium act. The property may consist of various kinds of development, such as a single high-rise structure, a number of garden apartment buildings, or a series of row houses. In every case, each condominium unit is identified in the declaration.

The purchaser of a condominium unit receives the fee simple to that unit and an undivided percentage interest in the common areas of the development as a tenant in common with the other unit owners. The common areas include the land and all aspects of the building not included within the description of individual condominium units. An owners association, usually formed as a corporation, manages the common areas and facilities.

The concept of individual ownership of part of a building has generated numerous legal problems. Litigation and legislation in the area is ever increasing. In 1977, the National Conference of Commissioners on Uniform State Laws approved the Uniform Condominium Act as a means to deal with unsettled condominium issues on a consistent basis throughout the country. Three years later the Commissioners amended and reissued the Act. The 1980 version of the Act has been enacted in a number of jurisdictions with modifications that vary among those states.

This book is designed to present the fundamentals of real estate finance, not an exhaustive analysis of condominium law. Hence, the remainder of this section treats only the narrow area of condominium financing.

B. FINANCING CONDOMINIUMS

1. Construction Financing

Condominium construction lending is in many respects similar to financing subdivision development. In each case, the developer obtains a blanket construction mortgage loan to finance the contemplated improvements. When construction is completed and a unit purchaser located, the purchaser obtains a permanent mortgage loan to pay the purchase price of the unit being acquired. The developer uses the money received from the purchaser to pay a proportionate share of the blanket construction loan. The construction lender in turn executes a partial release of the construction mortgage so that the developer can convey clear title to the unit in question. The end result is that the purchaser holds title to the unit subject only to the lien of the permanent purchase money mortgage. This process is repeated until no units are left in the hands of the developer. Thus, the transition from the construction loan to permanent financing is accomplished in a series of transactions as housing units in the subdivision or condominium are sold.

The condominium construction lender, however, faces a problem the subdivision financer does not. From a practical perspective, construction of the condominium building cannot be halted in midstream if the units not selling well. Further, if the lender executes a partial release as each unit is conveyed, the lender may end up with a lien on only the least valuable portions of its original security. Many condominium construction lenders, therefore, will not execute any partial releases until the developer has obtained sales contracts for a certain percentage of the units. The lender also may require the developer to have a plan for converting the development into a rental project in the event many units do not sell.

2. Conversion Financing

Owners of rental apartment buildings or other structures often convert their property to condominiums as a means to profitably dispose of real estate. The condominium conversion process presents some financing problems. The existing mortgagee may be unwilling to cooperate with the conversion and grant partial releases as the condominium units are sold. In this event, the owner must obtain short-term mortgage financing from another source in order to bridge the conversion period. The proceeds of the new mortgage loan are used to satisfy the original mortgage debt. The owner then organizes the condominium and sells the units. The transition from the interim loan to permanent financing is accomplished as described in the preceding section on construction financing.

3. Loans on Units

a. *General*

The owner of a condominium unit may obtain financing on the unit in the same manner as the owner of a single-family dwelling. Thus, there is not the same financial interdependence among condominium owners as exists among cooperative apartment members. If one condominium unit owner defaults in the payment of the unit owner's mortgage loan, the unit owner faces foreclosure alone. The lender does not necessarily have a lien on any other unit. This availability of separate financing of individual units is the most striking advantage of condominium ownership over investment in a cooperative apartment.

b. *Priority vis-à-vis Assessment Liens*

Although condominium unit owners are less financially interdependent than are cooperative apartment members, they are far more so than are homeowners in a typical subdivision. This is because unit owners must work together to maintain the condominium common areas. To achieve this objective, the condominium homeowners association makes an assessment against each unit owner for the unit owner's share of the expenses of the condominium project. If a unit owner does not pay the assessment, the association receives a statutory lien against the delinquent owner's condominium unit. Under many condominium statutes, a lien for unpaid assessments is junior to an existing first mortgage on the unit. The Uniform Condominium Act, however, gives an assessment lien priority over an existing first mortgage for up to six months of unpaid assessments on the ground that such a limited preference is crucial to the financial well-being of the development. *See* U.C.A. § 3–116. Mortgage lenders indirectly benefit from fully-funded maintenance programs because the value of their security is thereby preserved. Moreover, lenders may shield themselves against loss of lien priority by requiring the unit owner to escrow funds for assessments just as they often require the unit owner to place monies in escrow for real estate taxes and insurance. *See* Ch. 4, pp. 96–98 (discussing escrow accounts).

CHAPTER 12

REFORM

I. NEED FOR REFORM

The diverse real estate finance law discussed in the first eleven chapters of this book has impeded the free flow of funds for residential and commercial mortgage financing. Because national lenders must vary their procedures to meet a wide variety of state laws, the overall cost of administering mortgage loans is higher than if lenders had but one set of legal principles to follow. In addition, where mortgagees view local law as particularly burdensome, they tend to become more conservative in their lending practices and may even reduce their mortgage investments.

The current judicial foreclosure system is subject to especially heavy criticism. During the protracted, complex, and expensive court-supervised foreclosure process, mortgage money is tied up, and the mortgaged property may deteriorate or be destroyed, vandalized, or milked of its value.

II. REFORM MEASURES

In the latter part of the twentieth century and the initial years of the twenty-first century, various

236

sources advanced proposals to reform the law of real estate finance. *See* Ch. 10, p. 227 (noting response to 2007–2008 foreclosure escalation).

A.   FEDERAL LEVEL

1.   Nationwide Foreclosure System

Federal housing and secondary mortgage market programs are burdened by the absence of uniform state mortgage law. The 93rd Congress, therefore, entertained a bill to establish a standard nationwide procedure for foreclosing mortgages owned, insured, or guaranteed by an instrumentality of the federal government. This proposal, known as the Federal Mortgage Foreclosure Act, provided for nonjudicial foreclosure of all such federally related mortgages by a foreclosure commissioner. H.R. 10688, 93rd Cong., 1st Sess. (1973); S. 2507, 93rd Cong., 1st Sess. (1973). Although the Act was not adopted, it clearly demonstrated Congressional concern about the present fragmented state foreclosure system. Two decades later, the 104th Congress indicated a renewed interest in this issue by considering, but not adopting, a measure that would have authorized federal agencies to foreclose their mortgages by nonjudicial sale conducted by a foreclosure trustee. 141 Cong. Rec. H10745–H10748 (1995); 142 Cong. Rec. S3667–S3670 (1996).

Although a broad federal foreclosure system has not been enacted, twice Congress has passed narrow-gauged legislation on the subject. The Multifamily Mortgage Foreclosure Act of 1981, 12

U.S.C.A. § 3701 *et seq.*, establishes an out-of-court foreclosure system for certain multifamily mortgages held by the Department of Housing and Urban Development (HUD). A foreclosure commissioner is designated to conduct the procedure. The Single Family Mortgage Foreclosure Act of 1994, 12 U.S.C.A. § 3751 *et seq.*, creates a similar nonjudicial foreclosure scheme for certain "single-family" mortgages held by HUD.

2. Other Preemption

Certain federal statutes preempting state real estate finance law on nonforeclosure matters are addressed elsewhere in this book. Earlier chapters include discussion of qualified preemption of state usury law (*see* Ch. 4, p. 93), of state limitations on the use of alternative mortgage instruments (*see* Ch. 4, p. 86), and of state law regarding due-on-sale clauses (*see* Ch. 6, pp. 127–130). *See also* Ch. 2, pp. 50–51 (discussing predatory lending).

Federal regulatory bodies also have preempted state law on real estate finance through their regulation of lenders chartered by the federal government. An example of such preemption by regulation is considered in connection with due-on-sale clauses (*See* Ch. 6, p. 126). *See also* Ch. 2, pp. 50–51 (treating predatory lending).

The number of lawsuits brought by federal agencies challenging the applicability of local law to federally owned mortgages is another indication of the federal government's dissatisfaction with current mortgage law. In some of these cases, courts have found various state mortgage laws unenforceable against federal agencies on the ground that federal law or policy preempted the subject. State statutes establishing a statutory redemption period and limiting deficiency judgments are just two types of local laws that have met this fate.

3. Standard Mortgage Forms

Secondary mortgage market support institutions have brought a measure of uniformity to mortgage law and practice by standardizing mortgage forms. Fannie Mae (previously the Federal National Mortgage Association or FNMA) and Freddie Mac (previously the Federal Home Loan Mortgage Corporation or FHLMC) have developed uniform mortgage instruments with appropriate "riders." These uniform instruments are used widely.

4. Further Federal Action

Piecemeal federal legislation/regulation or sporadic litigation of the preemption issue is not an adequate substitute for a uniform mortgage law. Neither is the widespread use of standard mortgage forms. Consequently, Congress may continue to legislate on real estate finance matters and indeed, someday may adopt a wide-reaching system of out-of-court foreclosure. Whether such measures are ever enacted depends in part on the states. If they can agree on some uniformity in the real estate finance area, the impetus for further federal action to address mortgage law concerns may abate.

The federal government has become increasingly involved in the real estate finance arena of late. *See* Ch. 2, pp. 34–50 (tracing federal government involvement in financing process). The destabilized housing/mortgage market of 2007–2008 spawned extensive federal legislative and administrative activity. *See* Ch. 2, pp. 18–19 (introducing sources of real estate financing); Ch. 2, pp. 35–37 (analyzing mortgage insurance and guaranty programs); Ch. 2, pp. 37–39 (treating secondary mortgage market support institutions); Ch. 2, pp. 40–42 (discussing Truth in Lending); Ch. 2, pp. 48–49 (considering Housing and Economic Recovery Act of 2008); Ch. 2, pp. 49–50 (discussing Emergency Economic Stabilization Act of 2008); Ch. 10, p. 227 (noting response to 2007–2008 foreclosure escalation). Additional federal government involvement in the real estate financing process may lie shortly ahead. See Ch. 2, p. 50 (considering future involvement).

B.   UNIFORM LAND SECURITY INTEREST ACT

1.   General

The tool to achieve a unified real estate finance law among the states is available in the form of the Uniform Land Security Interest Act (ULSIA). Introduced originally in the mid–1970s as Article 3 of the Uniform Land Transactions Act, ULSIA was approved as a separate uniform act by the National Conference of Commissioners on Uniform State Laws in 1985.

ULSIA is designed to reform and unify the law governing real estate security arrangements through the adoption of personal property concepts embodied in the Uniform Commercial Code (UCC). ULSIA § 102. Modeled after Article 9 of the UCC,

ULSIA dramatically revises current real estate finance law. Although ULSIA deals in detail with a wide range of land financing problems, the scope of this work permits presentation of only its most significant aspects.

2. Significant Provisions

a. Coverage

With a few minor exceptions, ULSIA applies to every consensual arrangement that creates a security interest in realty. ULSIA §§ 102, 110. Thus, installment land contracts are treated the same as mortgages. *See* Ch. 3, pp. 60–67 (discussing installment land contract).

b. New Terminology and Concepts

ULSIA employs UCC-like terminology for traditional real estate financing concepts. Under the Act, mortgages are called security agreements, mortgagors are termed debtors, and mortgagees are labeled secured creditors. ULSIA § 111. ULSIA also establishes "protected party" status for residential mortgagors. ULSIA § 113. Protected parties receive special treatment in numerous ways, particularly in connection with foreclosure.

c. Rights and Obligations Before Foreclosure

ULSIA attempts to resolve many of the controversies that may arise between the parties before foreclosure. A major question in this area concerns the mortgagee's right to possess the mortgaged property. *See* Ch. 8, pp. 169–174 (analyzing significance of mortgage theories and discussing mortgagee in possession). ULSIA essentially adopts the intermediate mortgage theory, thereby permitting the mortgagee to take possession upon the mortgagor's default. ULSIA §§ 503, 505.

d. Foreclosure Procedures

ULSIA foreclosure provisions contain the reform of greatest interest to the real estate finance community. ULSIA §§ 506–514. Although foreclosure by judicial sale is still available in all cases, ULSIA recognizes and promotes power of sale foreclosure. Notice requirements for power of sale foreclosure, however, are more stringent than under existing out-of-court foreclosure schemes. *See* Ch. 10, pp. 217–222 (discussing foreclosure by power of sale). It is also noteworthy that ULSIA does not provide for a statutory redemption period. *See* Ch. 10, pp. 223–227 (considering statutory redemption).

3. Status

Although ULSIA and its ancestor, Article 3 of the Uniform Land Transactions Act, have generated considerable commentary in the legal literature, neither measure has been enacted anywhere. With the passage of time, the possibility that USLIA will be enacted in any jurisdiction is remote at best.

C. UNIFORM NONJUDICIAL FORECLOSURE ACT

The National Conference of Commissioners on Uniform State Laws continued its efforts to reform real estate finance law and in 2002 put forth a uniform act focused solely on foreclosure—the Uniform Nonjudicial Foreclosure Act (UNFA). This effort, as its title indicates, embraces out-of-court foreclosure. UNFA offers several possibilities in this regard: auction (UNFA §§ 301–311), negotiated sale (UNFA §§ 401–405), and appraisal—a variation of strict foreclosure (UNFA §§ 501–505). So far none of the states has enacted UNFA.

D.   RESTATEMENT (THIRD) OF PROPERTY—MORTGAGES

The American Law Institute, demonstrating concern about the current state of real estate finance law, undertook the task of preparing a restatement on the subject. The Restatement (Third) of Property—Mortgages was published in 1997. It presents an additional avenue for reform of the legal principles that govern land financing. *See* Ch. 7, pp. 156–157 (discussing subrogation for lender of pay-off funds).

TABLE OF SECONDARY AUTHORITIES

Secondary authorities are listed by section within each chapter. Certain sources cited in this table deserve special mention. My general approach to real estate finance has been significantly influenced by two casebooks: (1) the current and previous editions of Grant S. Nelson & Dale A. Whitman, Cases and Materials on Real Estate Transfer, Finance, and Development (7th ed. 2006) [hereinafter Nelson & Whitman casebook] and (2) an earlier edition of Norman Penney, Richard F. Broude, & Roger A. Cunningham, Cases and Materials on Land Financing (3d ed. 1985) [hereinafter Penney, Broude, & Cunningham]. Three other books served as key references: (1) Grant S. Nelson & Dale A. Whitman, Real Estate Finance Law (2 volume, Practitioner Treatise Series, 5th ed. 2007) [hereinafter Nelson & Whitman], (2) George E. Osborne, Handbook on the Law of Mortgages (2d ed. 1970) [hereinafter Osborne], and (3) Robert Kratovil & Raymond J. Werner, Modern Mortgage Law and Practice (2d ed. 1981) [hereinafter Kratovil & Werner].

CHAPTER 1. INTRODUCTION

I.   A.   1 Nelson & Whitman § 1.1.
     B.   Barlow Burke, Law of Title Insurance § 3.02[D] (3d ed. 2008); Kratovil & Werner § 32.01; 1 Nelson & Whitman §§ 5.27, 6.6.

C. Osborne §§ 49–64 (1st ed. 1951 & 2d ed. 1970); 4 Richard R. Powell, Powell on Real Property § 37.19 (Michael Allan Wolf gen. ed., 2008) [hereinafter Powell]; 5 Herbert T. Tiffany & Basil Jones, The Law of Real Property § 1563 (3d ed. 1939 & Cum. Supp. Sept. 2007).

II. Kratovil & Werner §§ 1.2–1.5, 1.7, 3.01, 41.08–41.08(a)(1), 41.09, 41.10; 1 Nelson & Whitman §§ 1.1–1.4, 1.6–1.7, 3.1–3.2, 7.1, 7.9–7.11, 7.19, 8.4; Osborne §§ 5–10, 311; 4 Powell §§ 37.02, 37.36; Howard E. Kane, *The Mortgagee's Option to Purchase Mortgaged Property* in Financing Real Estate in the 80s 123, 127–139 (Brian J. Strum ed., 1981) (reference for section B.2. only); Jeffrey L. Licht, *The Clog on the Equity of Redemption and Its Effect on Modern Real Estate Finance,* 60 St. John's L.Rev. 452 (1986) (reference for sections A. & B. only); John C. Murray, *Clogging Revisited,* 33 Real Prop., Prob. & Tr. J. 279 (1998) (reference for section B.2. only). ; Morris G. Shanker, *Will Mortgage Law Survive? A Commentary and Critique on Mortgage Law's Birth, Long Life, and Current Proposals for Its Demise,* 54 Case W.Res. L.Rev. 69 (2003) (reference for sections A. & B. only).

III. Kratovil & Werner §§ 1.6, 1.8, 20.02; 1 Nelson & Whitman §§ 1.5, 4.1–4.3; Osborne §§ 13–16.

CHAPTER 2. MORTGAGE MARKET

I. A. & B. 1. & 2. Robert Kratovil, Modern Mortgage Law and Practice §§ 207–209 (1972) [hereinafter Kratovil (1972)]; Kratovil & Werner §§ 25.05–25.11, 25.35–25.38(a); 2 Nelson & Whitman § 12.1; Nelson & Whitman casebook 888.

3. a. & b. 1 Alvin A. Arnold & Marshall E. Tracht, Construction and Development Financing §§ 4:151–4:164, 4:177–4:179 (3d ed. 2001 & Oct. 2008 Supp.) [hereinafter Arnold & Tracht]; Kratovil & Werner §§ 25.03–25.03(b)(2), 25.13, 25.17–25.21, 25.27(f)–25.27(f)(5); 1 Michael T. Madison, Jeffrey R. Dwyer, & Steven W. Bender, The Law of Real Estate Financing §§ 6:20, 6:24 (revised ed. 2008–Release No. 14) [hereinafter Madison, Dwyer, & Bender]; 2 Nelson & Whitman §§ 12.1–12.2; B.C. Hart & Howard E. Kane, *What Every Real Estate Lawyer Should Know About Payment and Performance Bonds,* 17 Real Prop., Prob. & Tr.J. 674 (1982); Colin C. Livingston, *Current Business Approaches–Commercial Construction Lending,* 13 Real Prop., Prob. & Tr.J. 791 (1978).

c. 1 Arnold & Tracht § 4:262; 1 Madison, Dwyer, & Bender § 6:52; 2 Nelson & Whitman § 12.11; Cindy A. Ferguson,

        Lender's Liability for Construction Defects, 11 Real Est.L.J. 310 (1983); Comment, *Liability of the Institutional Lender for Structural Defects in New Housing,* 35 U.Chi.L.Rev. 739 (1968); Craig R. Thorstenson, Note, *Mortgage Lender Liability to the Purchasers of New or Existing Homes,* 1988 U.Ill. L.Rev. 191.

    C. Nelson & Whitman casebook 888–889.

II. D. Barlow Burke, Jr., Law of Federal Mortgage Documents §§ 7.4.2–7.5 (1989 & Supp. 1995); 2 Nelson & Whitman § 11.1; Nelson & Whitman casebook 495–496, 886–888.

III. Allan Axelrod, Curtis J. Berger, & Quintin Johnstone, Land Transfer and Finance Cases and Materials 113–121, Supp. 12–15 (3d ed. 1986 & Supp. 1991); Curtis J. Berger, Quintin Johnstone, & Marshall Tracht, Land Transfer and Finance Cases and Materials 102–104, 106–107 (5th ed. 2007); Kratovil & Werner §§ 7.03(d)–7.03(e), 32.11; Madison, Dwyer, & Bender xxxii–xlii (Release 4, July 2003); 1 Madison, Dwyer, & Bender, xi–xxxvi, §§ 3:8–3:11, 3:25–3:27, 3:29; 1 Nelson & Whitman § 5.28; 2 Nelson & Whitman §§ 11.1, 11.3; 4 Pt.1 Patrick J. Rohan, Real Estate Financing § 3.01 (1996) [hereinafter Rohan]; Caryl A. Yzenbaard, Residential Real Estate Transactions § 4:5 (2005); U.S. Dept. of Hous. & Urb. Dev. Report, Housing in the Seventies 68–73, 140–145, 152–155 (1974) [hereinafter HUD Report]; Barbara Miles, *Housing Finance: Development and Evolution in Mortgage Markets* in Housing–A Reader 45, 55–65 (Cong. Research Service, Library of Congress, July, 1983) [hereinafter Miles]; Raymond H. Brescia, *Capital in Chaos: The Subprime Mortgage Crisis and the Social Capital Response,* 56 Clev. St. L.Rev. 271 (2008); Peter J. Hong & Marcos Reza, *Hidden Costs to Homeowners: The Prevalent Non–Disclosure of Yield Spread Premiums in Mortgage Loan Transactions,* 18 Loy. Consumer L. Rev. 131 (2005); Howell E. Jackson & Laurie Burlingame, *Kickbacks or Compensation: The Case of Yield Spread Premiums,* 12 Stan. J.L. Bus. & Fin. 289 (2007); Leonard Sahling & Elizabeth Lavin, *Will RTC Asset Dispositions Ruin the Real Estate Markets?,* Real Est. Rev., Summer 1990, at 15; David Schmudde, *Lessons from the Subprime Mortgage Debacle,* Prac. Real Est.Law., May 2008, at 9; Vikas Bajaj, *Housing Lenders Fear Bigger Wave of Loan Defaults,* N.Y. Times, Aug. 4, 2008, at A1; Michael Corkery, Jonathan Karp, & Damian Paletta, *Real-Estate Woes of Banks Mount,* Wall St.J., June 6, 2008, at 1; Mark Maremont, *Mortgage-Market Trouble Reaches Big Credit Unions,* Wall St.J., Aug. 11, 2008, at 1; *RTC Raises $404 Million in Final Loan Auctions,* Housing & Dev. Rep., 23 Current Dev. 533 (Jan. 1, 1996); *Survey of Mortgage Lending Activity–1988,* HUD News Release, April 12, 1989; *Survey of Mortgage Lending Activity–Fourth Quarter/Annual, 1995,* HUD News Release, April 26, 1996.

IV. Kratovil & Werner §§ 4.01–4.06; 2 Nelson & Whitman §§ 11.5, 12.3; Penney, Broude, & Cunningham 756–757; 4 Powell § 37.09 ; L. Travis Brannon, Jr., *Enforceability of Mortgage Loan Commitments,* 18 Real Prop., Prob. & Tr.J. 724 (1983); Roger D. Groot, *Specific Performance of Contracts to Provide Permanent Financing,*

60 Cornell L.Rev. 718 (1975); Michael Krimminger, *"It's Alive!"*— *Mortgage Risk Reborn: Issues and Possible Solutions*, 17 J. Affordable Housing & Community Dev. L. 259 (2008); Dustin Fisher, Comment, *Selling the Payments: Predatory Lending Goes Primetime*, 41 J. Marshall L.Rev. 587 (2008).

V. Kratovil & Werner §§ 29.04–29.04(c), 33.01–33.10(c); 1 Madison, Dwyer, & Bender §§ 4:36–4:57; 2 Madison, Dwyer, & Bender §§ 11:1–11:2; 1 Nelson & Whitman § 5.35; 2 Nelson & Whitman § 11.3; Andrew Lance, *Balancing Private and Public Initiatives in the Mortgage–Backed Security Market*, 18 Real Prop., Prob. & Tr.J. 426 (1983); Walter M. Strine, Jr., *New Commercial Devices— Mortgage–Backed Securities,* 13 Real Prop., Prob. & Tr.J. 1011 (1978).

VI.   A. Nelson & Whitman casebook 995; 4C Rohan §§ 9A.01, 9A.02[1]–[2], 9A.03[1]–[2] (1996); 5A Rohan Ch. 9A Scope, § 9A.05[1]–[2] (2007); Julia Patterson Forrester, *Mortgaging the American Dream: A Critical Evaluation of the Federal Government's Promotion of Home Equity Financing*, 69 Tul.L.Rev. 373 (1994).

    B. Kratovil & Werner §§ 24.11–24.11(f); 1 Nelson & Whitman § 9.8; Nelson & Whitman casebook 867–885; 5A Rohan § 9A.05[3] (2007); Francis P. Gunning, *The Wrap– Around Mortgage . . . Friend or U.F.O.?,* 2 Real Est.Rev. 35 (Summer 1972); Note, *Wrap–Around Financing: A Technique for Skirting the Usury Laws?,* 1972 Duke L.J. 785; Bill B. Caraway, Note, *Unwrapping the Wraparound Mortgage Foreclosure Process,* 47 Wash. & Lee L.Rev. 1025 (1990).

VII.   A. HUD Report 11–17, 83–137; Grace Milgram, *Housing the Urban Poor: Urban Housing Assistance Programs* in Housing–A Reader 114 (Cong.Research Service, Library of Congress, July 1983).

    B. HUD Report 78–81; 2 Nelson & Whitman § 11.2; 4A Rohan §§ 2E.01–2E.25 (2007); 4C Rohan §§ 3I.18–3I.19, 3I.27 (2007); Miles 61; Quintin Johnstone, *Private Mortgage Insurance,* 39 Wake Forest L.Rev. 783 (2004); Joseph E. Mayk, *The Private Mortgage Insurance Law–An Answer with More Questions?,* 53 Consumer Fin. L.Q. Rep. 168 (1999); 2 Housing & Development Reporter 11:0011–11:0014 (2002); S. Rep. No. 110–227 (2007); David M. Herszenhorn, *Senate Passes Housing Legislation That Raises the Nation's Debt Limit,* N.Y. Times, July 27, 2008, at 16; *The Housing Bill,* N.Y. Times, July 27, 2008, at 16; Damian Paletta, *Bush Signs Housing– Relief Bill Into Law,* Wall St.J., Aug. 4, at A3; *Regulations Issued to Implement New FHA Mortgage Refinancing Program for Troubled Homeowners,* 36 No. CD–20 HDR Current Developments 2 (Oct. 13, 2008).

    C. HUD Report 62–64, 73–78; 2 Nelson & Whitman § 11.3; Miles 59–61; James R. Hagerty, Deborah Soloman, & Sudeep Reddy, *Treasury, Fed Affirm Backing for Ailing Mortgage Giants,* Wall St.J., July 14, 2008, at A1; Stephen Labaton, *Treasury Unveils Vast Plan to Save Mortgage Giants,* N.Y. Times, July 14, 2008, at A1; David M. Herszenhorn, *Senate Passes Housing Legislation That Raises the Nation's Debt Limit,* N.Y. Times, July 27, 2008, at 16; *The Housing Bill*, N.Y. Times, July 27, 2008, at 16; Damian Paletta, *Bush Signs Housing–Relief Bill Into Law*, Wall St.J., Aug. 4, at A3; James R. Hagerty, Ruth Simon, & Damian Paletta, *U.S. Seizes Mortgage Giants*, Wall St.J., Sept. 8, 2008, at 1; Stephen Labaton & Edmund L. Andrews, *In Rescue, U.S. Takes Over Mortgage Finance Titans: A Costly Bailout*, N.Y. Times, Sept. 8, 2008, at A1.

D.　　1. 1 Paul Barron, Michael A. Berenson, & Dan Rosin, Federal Regulation of Real Estate and Mortgage Lending §§ 10:1–10:87 (4th ed. 2008 & June 2008 Cum.Supp.) [hereinafter Barron & Berenson]; David G. Epstein & Steve H. Nickles, Consumer Law in a Nutshell 80–85, 138–146, 198–201 (2d ed. 1981) [hereinafter Epstein & Nickles]; 4 Powell § 37A.01; Jo Carrillo, *Dangerous Loans: Consumer Challenges to Adjustable Rate Mortgages*, 5 Berkeley Bus.L.J. 1 (2008); Gary Klein, *Preventing Home Equity Lending Fraud: Special Truth in Lending Protections Enacted*, 7 Loy. Consumer L.Rep. 126 (1995); Stephen F.J. Ornstein, *Examining the Effect of New Legislation on Consumer Protection for "High Cost Mortgages,"* 25 Real Est.L.J. 40 (1996); Sepideh "Sepi" C. Khansari & Kathryn Reed Edge, *Changes to HOEPA Regulations*, Real Est. Fin.J., Fall 2008, at 52; Jeffrey Taft & Maya Wilson, *Federal Reserve Board Issues Final Rule Addressing Mortgage Lending and Servicing Practices Under Regulation Z*, Real Est.Fin.J., Fall 2008, at 81; Truth in Lending, 73 Fed. Reg. 44,522 (July 30, 2008); *The Housing Bill*, N.Y. Times, July 27, 2008, at 16.

　　2. 1 Barron, Berenson, & Rosin §§ 3:1–3:100; Epstein & Nickles 146–149; Frank E. Catalina, *From the Legislatures: Interstate Land Sales— Tightening Consumer Protection*, 10 Real Est. L.J. 72 (1981); Robin Paul Malloy, *The Interstate Land Sales Full Disclosure Act: Its Requirements, Consequences, and Implications for Persons Participating in Real Estate Development*, 24 B.C.L.Rev. 1187 (1983); Report of Comm. on Regulation of Land Sales, Real Prop. Div., *Exemptions from the Registration Requirements of the Interstate Land Sales Full Disclosure Act*, 15 Real Prop., Prob. & Tr.J. 334 (1980); Ronald A. Johnston, Comment, *The Interstate Land Sales Full Disclosure Act: An Analysis of Administrative Policies Implemented in the Years 1968– 1975*, 26 Cath.U.L.Rev. 348 (1977); Ralph Bellar, Jr., Comment, *Regulating the Real Estate Indus*

try: The Problem of Dual Registration, 37 U.Kan. L.Rev. 145 (1988).

3. 1 Madison, Dwyer, & Bender § 5:57; Michael S. Baram & J. Raymond Miyares, *Managing Flood Risk: Technical Uncertainty in the National Flood Insurance Program,* 7 Colum.J.Envt.L. 129 (1982); Leonard A. Bernstein, Phillip H. Myers, & Daniel Steen, *Flood Insurance Reform Act Engulfs Mortgage Lenders,* 112 Banking L.J. 238 (1995); Niles S. Campbell, *Regulators to Issue Flood Regulations; OCC Outlines Flood Insurance Guidelines,* 65:12 BNA Banking Report 529 (Oct. 2, 1995); Marilyn Cane & Paul A. Caldarelli, *Apres le Deluge: National Flood Insurance,* 17 Nova L.Rev. 1077 (1993); Oliver A. Houck, *Rising Water: The National Flood Insurance Program and Louisiana,* 60 Tul.L.Rev. 61 (1985); Malcolm K. Montgomery & Francis P. Lively, *The Rising Tide—Flood Insurance in an Active Hurricane Era,* Real Est.Fin.J., Winter 2007, at 63; Rod Sands, *A Refresher on Federal Flood Hazard Insurance Requirements,* Prac. Real Est. Law., March 1995, at 85; Adam F. Scales, *A Nation of Policyholders: Governmental and Market Failure in Flood Insurance,* 26 Miss. C.L.Rev. 3 (2006); David E. Sturgess & John P. McHugh, *Flood Hazard Insurance: Requirements Imposed on Banks Extending Loans Secured by Real Property,* 16 Real Est.L.J. 226 (1988); Gerald M. Tierney, *The National Flood Insurance Program: Explanation and Legal Implications,* 8 Urb.Law 279 (1976); Bryant J. Spann, Note, *Going Down for the Third Time: Senator Kerry's Reform Bill Could Save the Drowning National Flood Insurance Program,* 28 Ga.L.Rev. 593 (1994); Charles T. Griffith, Note, *The National Flood Insurance Program: Unattained Purposes, Liability in Contract, and Takings,* 35 Wm. & Mary L.Rev. 727 (1994); H.R. Rep. No. 110–340 (2007); *House Passes Flood Insurance Bill with Coverage for Wind Damage,* 35 No. CD–20 HDR Current Developments 16 (Oct. 15, 2007); S. Rep. No. 110–214 (2007); *Sens. Dodd, Shelby Laud Senate Passage of Flood Legislation,* US Fed News, May 13, 2008; *Senate Passes Flood Insurance Bill After Rejecting Amendment to Add Coverage for Wind Damage,* 36 No. CD–10 HDR Current Developments 5 (May 19, 2008).

4. 1 Barron, Berenson, & Rosin §§ 2:1–2:119; Epstein & Nickles 149–151; 4 Powell § 37A.02; Charles G. Field, *RESPA in a Nutshell,* 11 Real Prop., Prob. & Tr.J. 447 (1976); Eloisa C. Rodri-

guez–Dod, *RESPA–Questioning Its Effectiveness*, 24 Hamline L. Rev. 68 (2000).

5. 1 Barron, Berenson, & Rosin §§ 11:1–11:34; Alfred J. Lechner, Jr., *National Banks and State Anti–Redlining Laws: Has Congress Preempted the Field?*, 99 Banking L.J. 388 (1982); Richard D. Marsico, *Fighting Poverty Through Community Empowerment and Economic Development: The Role of the Community Reinvestment and Home Mortgage Disclosure Acts*, 12 N.Y.L.Sch. J.Hum.Rts. 281 (1995); Barbara A. Kleinman & Katherine Sloss Berger, Note, *The Home Mortgage Disclosure Act of 1975: Will It Protect Urban Consumers from Redlining?*, 12 N.Eng. L.Rev. 957 (1977).

6. 2 Madison, Dwyer, & Bender §§ 14:39–14:45; 4 Pt.1 Rohan, Special Alert, *Summary of Lender Liability Legislation* (1996); Monika Cornell, *Environmental Insurance: An Option to a Phase I Environmental Site Assessment,* Real Est.Fin.J., Winter 2003 at 24; Paul A. Dominick & Leon C. Harmon, *Lender Limbo: The Perils of Environmental Lender Liability,* 41 S.C.L.Rev. 855 (1990); Jack Fersko & Ann M. Waeger, *Using Environmental Insurance in Commercial Real Estate Transactions*, Prob. & Prop., Jan./Feb. 2003, at 30; Marianne M. Jennings, *Lender Liability, CERCLA, and Other Things That Go Bump in the Night*, 24 Real Est.L.J. 372 (1996); Paul Katcher, *Lenders' Liability for Environmental Hazards,* 20:3 Real Est.Rev. 72 (Fall 1990); Michael B. Kupin, *New Alterations of the Lender Liability Landscape: CERCLA After The "Fleet Factors" Decision,* 19 Real Est.L.J. 191 (1991); Michael P. Last, *Superfund Liability Traps Affecting Developers and Lenders,* 3:3 Nat.Resources & Env't. 10 (Fall 1988); Roger J. Marzulla & Brett G. Kappel, *Lender Liability Under the Comprehensive Environmental Response, Compensation and Liability Act,* 41 S.C.L.Rev. 705 *and Money: How Environmental Lender Liability Changed the Leopards' Spots*, 25 Real Est.L.J. 56 (1996); Lawrence P. Schnapf, *Lender Liability Today Under Environmental Laws*, 60 Consumer Fin. L.Q. Rep. 147 (2006); John M. Van Lieshout, *Bankers Beware: Liability of Lending Institutions Under Superfund,* 2 Hofstra Prop.L.J. 291 (1989); Alan P. Vollmann, *Double Jeopardy: Lender Liability Under Superfund,* 16 Real Est. L.J. 3 (1987); David J. Portelli, Comment, *SARA Slams the Door: The Effect of Superfund Amendments on Foreclosing Mortgagees,* 34 Wayne

L.Rev. 223 (1987); Kathleen Hellevik, *Spending Package Contains Provision Clarifying Lender Liability for Cleanup of Contaminated Real Estate*, 10–11–96 WLN 10807.

7. David M. Herszenhorn, *Senate Passes Housing Legislation That Raises the Nation's Debt Limit*, N.Y. Times, July 27, 2008, at 16; *The Housing Bill*, N.Y. Times, July 27, 2008, at 16; Damian Paletta, *Bush Signs Housing–Relief Bill Into Law*, Wall St.J., Aug. 4, at A3.

8. Greg Hitt & Sarah Lueck, *Senate Expands Bailout Package*, Wall St.J., Oct. 2, 2008, at A3; David M. Herszenhorn, *Bailout Plan Wins Approval; Democrats Vow Tighter Rules: Bush Signs Bill*, N.Y. Times, Oct. 4, 2008, at A1; Mark Landler & Edmund L. Andrews, *Bailout Plan Wins Approval; Democrats Vow Tighter Rules: For Treasury Dept., Now Come the Hard Part*, N.Y. Times, Oct. 4, 2008, at A1; Greg Hitt & Deborah Solomon, *Bush Signs Bailout Bill As Economy Slips Further*, Wall St.J., Oct. 4–5, 2008, at 1; Edmund L. Andrews & Mark Landler, *U.S. May Take Ownership Stake in Banks to Ease Credit Crisis: Injection of Cash*, N.Y. Times, Oct. 9, at A1; Mark Landler & Edmund L. Andrews, *Nations Weighing Global Approach As Chaos Spreads*, N.Y. Times, Oct. 10, at A1; Steve Lohr, *U.S. Investing $250 Billion To Bolster Bank Industry; Dow Surges 936 Points: Bold Action With Basis in History*, N.Y. Times, Oct. 14, 2008, at 1A; Deborah Solomon, Damian Paletta, Michael M. Phillips, & Jon Hilsenrath, *U.S. to Buy Stakes in Nation's Largest Banks*, Wall St.J., Oct. 14, 2008, at 1; Deborah Solomon & David Enrich, *Devil Is in Bailout's Details*, Wall St.J., Oct. 15, 2008, at 1; *A New Set of Tools*, Wall St.J., Oct. 15, 2008, at A16; http://thomas. loc.gov/ (follow "Public Laws" hyperlink; then follow "110–301–110–343" hyperlink to "343.") (last visited Oct. 7, 2008).

9. James R. Hagerty, Ruth Simon, & Damian Paletta, *U.S. Seizes Mortgage Giants*, Wall St.J., Sept. 8, 2008, at 1; Stephen Labaton & Edmund L. Andrews, *In Rescue, U.S. Takes Over Mortgage Finance Titans: A Costly Bailout*, N.Y. Times, Sept. 8, 2008, at A1. David M. Herszenhorn, *Bailout Plan Wins Approval; Democrats Vow Tighter Rules: Bush Signs Bill*, N.Y. Times, Oct. 4, 2008, at A1; Edmund L. Andrews & Mark Landler, *U.S. May Take Ownership Stake in Banks to Ease Credit Crisis: Injection of Cash*, N.Y. Times, Oct. 9, at A1.

VIII. 1 Nelson & Whitman § 5.30; 2 Nelson & Whitman §§ 11.5-11.6; Kathleen C. Engle & Patricia A. McCoy, *A Tale of Three Markets: The Law and Economics of Predatory Lending*, 80 Texas L. Rev. 1255 (2002); Julia Patterson Forrester, *Still Mortgaging the American Dream: Predatory Lending, Preemption, and Federally Supported Lenders*, 74 U.Cin.L.Rev. 1303 (2006); Celest M. Hammond, *Predatory Lending—A Legal Definition and Update*, 34 Real Est. L.J. 176 (2005); Lisa Keyfetz, *The Home Ownership and Equity Protection Act of 1994: Extending Liability for Predatory Subprime Loans to Secondary Mortgage Market Participants*, 18 Loy. Consumer L.Rev. 151 (2005); Richard D. Marsico, *Subprime Lending, Predatory Lending, and the Community Reinvestment Act: Obligations of Banks*, 46 N.Y.L.Sch.L.Rev. 735 (2003); Debra Pogrund Stark, *Unmasking the Predatory Loan in Sheep's Clothing: A Legislative Proposal*, 21 Harv. BlackLetter L.J. 129 (2005); Tania Davenport, Note, *An American Nightmare: Predatory Lending in the Subprime Home Mortgage Industry*, 36 Suffolk U. L.Rev. 531 (2003); Dustin Fisher, Comment, *Selling the Payments: Predatory Lending Goes Primetime*, 41 J. Marshall L.Rev. 587 (2008); Donita Judge, Note, *Predatory Lending: Legalized Theft of Home Equity*, 5 Rutgers Race & L.Rev. 293 (2003); Abraham B. Putney, Note, *Rules, Standards, and Suitability: Finding the Correct Approach to Predatory Lending*, 71 Fordham L.Rev. 2101 (2003); Michael J. Pyle, Comment, *A "Flip" Look at Predatory Lending: Will the Fed's Revised Regulation Z End Abusive Refinancing Practices?*, 112 Yale L.J. 1919 (2003); *New York, Georgia Fair Lending Laws Preempted by Federal Statute, OTS Rules*, 71 U.S.L.W. 2503 (2003); *Attorneys General, Activists Decry OCC Rules on Preemption of Predatory Lending Laws*, 72 U.S.L.W. 2199 (2003); *OCC Releases Final Preemption Regulations; Spitzer Says Change Cannot Deter Lawsuits*, 72 U.S.L.W. 2390 (2004).

CHAPTER 3. REAL ESTATE FINANCING DEVICES

I.   A. Kratovil & Werner §§ 19.01–19.09; 1 Nelson & Whitman §§ 1.1, 9.1.
      B. Mark Lee Levine & Libbi Levine Seger, Real Estate Transactions—Tax Planning and Consequences (2008 ed.); 2 Madison, Dwyer, & Bender §§ 12:85–12:98; Michael T. Madison & Jeffrey R. Dwyer, The Law of Real Estate Financing ¶¶ 12.01–12.02 (1981 & Cum. Supp. 1993).

II.   Kratovil & Werner §§ 3.01–3.03(g); 1 Nelson & Whitman §§ 1.6, 7.19; Nelson & Whitman casebook 630–631; Osborne § 17.

III. Kratovil & Werner §§ 3.04–3.08; 1 Nelson & Whitman §§ 3.1–3.19, 3.39; 4 Powell §§ 37.17–37.20, 37.21[2]–[3]; Roger A. Cunningham & Saul Tischler, *Disguised Real Estate Security Transactions as Mortgages in Substance*, 26 Rutgers L.Rev. 1 (1972); Jeffrey A. Grabowski, *Lender Beware: Unrecorded Vendee Liens Threaten Loan Priority*, Real Est. Fin. J., Winter 2001, at 56; Comment Note, *Different Classes of "Vendors' Liens," So–Called, Upon Real Property*, 91 A.L.R. 148 (1934); W. R. Habeeb, Annotation, *Right of Vendee Under Executory Land Contract to Lien for Amount Paid on Purchase Price*, 33 A.L.R.2d 1384 (1954).

IV.   A. & B. 1 Nelson & Whitman §§ 3.26–3.34, 3.38; 1 Nelson & Whitman § 3.34 (3d ed. 1994); Osborne § 20; Penney,

Broude & Cunningham 544–549; 4 Powell § 37.21[1]; Eric T. Freyfogle, *Vagueness and the Rule of Law: Reconsidering Installment Land Contract Forfeitures,* 1988 Duke L.J. 609; John R. Lewis & John R. Reeves, *How the Doctrine of Equitable Conversion Affects Land Sale Contract Forfeitures,* 3 Real Est.L.J. 249 (1974); Allen E. Korpela, Annotation, *Specific Performance of Land Contract Notwithstanding Failure of Vendee to Make Required Payments on Time,* 55 A.L.R.3d 10 (1974).

C. 1 Nelson & Whitman § 3.35; William M. Casey, Comment, *Real Estate Contracts—When Recording of a Lien Instrument is Not Notice to the Whole World—Actual Notice Required to Protect Second Lien on a Real Estate Contract:* Shindledecker v. Savage, 13 N.M.L.Rev. 177 (1983); Thomas A. Henzler, Recent Case, *Mortgages—Mortgage of a Vendee's Interest in an Installment Land Contract—Mortgagee's Rights Upon Default,* 43 Mo.L.Rev. 371 (1978); Recent Development, *Mortgages—Notice—Vendor and Purchaser—Vendor Not Charged With Constructive Notice of Subsequent Mortgage of Contract Purchaser's Equity—Mortgage Required to Notify Vendor to Protect Security Interest.* —Kendrick v. Davis, 75 Wash. Dec. 2d 470, 452 P.2d 222 (1969), 45 Wash. L. Rev. 645 (1970).

D. 1 Nelson & Whitman § 3.37; Nelson & Whitman casebook 328–330; Larry M. Wertheim, *Revised Article 9 of the U.C.C. and Minnesota Contracts for Deed,* 28 Wm. Mitchell L. Rev. 1483 (2002); Dale A. Whitman, *Transfers by Vendors of Interests in Installment Land Contracts: The Impact of Revised Article 9 of the Uniform Commercial Code,* 38 Real Prop., Prob. & Tr.J. 421 (2003).

V. A. & B. Kratovil & Werner §§ 20.10–20.11, 21.01–22.26, 30.07; 1 Milton R. Friedman, & Patrick J. Randolph, Jr., Friedman on Leases §§ 7:1–7:3.2[E], 7:8–7:8.3, 8:4 (2008); Nelson & Whitman casebook 1179–1182; Grant S. Nelson & Dale A. Whitman, Cases and Materials on Real Estate Finance and Development 972, 985–986 (1976); 5A Rohan §§ 7.01–7.06, 7A.01–7A.06 (2007); Jesse B. Heath, Jr., *Sale–Leasebacks and Leasehold Mortgages* in Financing Real Estate in the 80s 141 (Brian J. Strum ed., 1981); Martin Kobren, *Three Perspectives on Ground Lease Negotiations* 19 Real Est.L.J. 40 (1990); Report of Comm. on Leases, *Ground Leases and Their Financing,* 4 Real Prop., Prob. & Tr. J. 437 (1969).

C. Kratovil & Werner §§ 23.01–23.08; 5 Rohan §§ 6.01–6.05 (2007); Jesse B. Heath, Jr., *Sale–Leasebacks and Leasehold Mortgages* in Financing Real Estate in the 80s 141 (Brian J. Strum ed., 1981); Thomas C. Homburger & Gregory R. Andre, *Real Estate Sale and Leasebacks Transactions and the Risk of Recharacterization in Bankruptcy Proceedings,* 24 Real Prop., Prob. & Tr.J. 95 (1989); Thomas C. Homburger & Karl L. Marschel, *Recharacterization Revisted: A View of Recharacterization of Sale and Leaseback Transactions in Bankruptcy After Fifteen Years,* 41 Real Prop., Prob. & Tr.J. 123 (2006).

VI. 2 Madison, Dwyer, & Bender §§ 8:20–8:24; Andrew R. Berman, *Risks and Realities of Mezzanine Loans*, 72 Mo.L.Rev. 993 (2007); Andrew R. Berman, *"Once a Mortgage, Always a Mortgage"—The Use (and Misuse of) Mezzanine Loans and Preferred Equity Investments*, 11 Stan.J.L.,Bus. & Fin. 76 (2005); Robert G. Koen & Gary A. Goodman, *Mezzanine Loans Now a Key Commercial Real Estate Financing Option*, Real Est.Fin.J., Summer 2002, at 20; John C. Murray & Randall L. Scott, *Title and UCC Insurance for Mezzanine–Financing Transactions*, 43 Real Prop., Tr. & Est.L.J. 83 (2008); Richard R. Goldberg, *Perfection of Security Interests in the Ownership Interests of Borrowers Under a Mezzanine Loan: Article 9 vs. Article 8*, Prob. & Prop., Sept./Oct. 2008, at 14.

CHAPTER 4. UNDERLYING OBLIGATION

I.–II. Kratovil & Werner §§ 10.01–10.07; 1 Nelson & Whitman §§ 2.1–2.3; Frank A. St. Claire, *Nonrecourse Debt Transactions: Limitations on Limitations of Liability*, 19 Real Est.L.J. 19 (1990); Gregory M. Stein, *The Scope of the Borrower's Liability in a Nonrecourse Real Estate Loan*, 55 W. & L. L.Rev. 1207 (1998); U.C.C. § 3–106 cmt. 1 (2007); U.C.C. § 3–105 cmts. 3–4 (1972).

III. Kratovil & Werner §§ 10.08–10.08(c); 1 Nelson & Whitman § 2.4; Osborne § 106.

IV. A. Osborne § 114; Grant S. Nelson & Dale A. Whitman, *Rethinking Future Advance Mortgages: A Brief for the Restatement Approach*, 44 Duke L.J. 657 (1995) [hereinafter Nelson & Whitman, *Rethinking Future Advance Mortgages*].

   B. Kratovil & Werner §§ 11.01, 11.05; 2 Nelson & Whitman § 12.7.

   C. 2 Grant Gilmore, Security Interests in Personal Property § 35.4 (1965) [hereinafter Gilmore]; Kratovil & Werner §§ 11.02–11.12; 2 Nelson & Whitman § 12.7; Osborne § 119; James B. Hughes, Jr., *Future Advance Mortgages: Preserving the Benefits and Burdens of the Bargain*, 29 Wake Forest L.Rev. 1101 (1994); Robert Kratovil & Raymond J. Werner, *Mortgages for Construction and the Lien Priorities Problem— The "Unobligatory" Advance*, 41 Tenn.L.Rev. 311 (1974) [hereinafter Kratovil & Werner, *Mortgages for Construction*]; Nelson & Whitman, *Rethinking Future Advance Mortgages;* Benjamin E. Griffith & Crane Davis Kipp, Comment, *Mortgages to Secure Future Advances: Problems of Priority and the Doctrine of Economic Necessity,* 46 Miss.L.J. 433 (1975).

   D. 2 Nelson & Whitman § 12.7; Restatement (Third) of Property: Mortgages § 2.1, *Statutory Note on Future Advances* (1997); Nelson & Whitman, *Rethinking Future Advance Mortgages*.

   E. 2 Gilmore, § 35.4; Kratovil & Werner § 25.12; 1 Madison, Dwyer, & Bender § 6:16; 2 Nelson & Whitman § 12.7; Robert Kratovil, *Mortgage Priority Problems: The New Illinois Mortgage Foreclosure Act and the Impact of the Uniform Acts,* 8 N.Ill.U.L.Rev. 1 (1987); Kratovil & Werner, *Mortgages for Construction;* Nelson & Whitman, *Rethinking Future Advance Mortgages;* Larry Skipworth, *Should Construction Lenders Lose Out On Voluntary Advances If a Loan Turns Sour?,* 5 Real Est.L.J. 221 (1977); Benjamin E. Griffith & Crane Davis Kipp, Comment, *Mortgages to Secure Future Advances: Prob lems of Priority and the Doctrine of Economic Necessity,* 46 Miss.L.J. 433 (1975).

F. 2 Gilmore § 35.2; Kratovil & Werner § 10.11; 2 Nelson & Whitman § 12.8; Nelson & Whitman, *Rethinking Future Advance Mortgages;* Milton Roberts, Annotation, *Debts Included in Provision of Mortgage Purporting to Cover All Future and Existing Debts (Dragnet Clause)—Modern Status,* 3 A.L.R.4th 690 (1981); P. H. Vartanian, Annotation, *Debts Included in Provision of Mortgage Purporting to Cover Unspecified Future or Existing Debts ("Dragnet" Clause),* 172 A.L.R. 1079 (1948).

V. A. 1 Nelson & Whitman § 1.1; Nelson & Whitman casebook 981–985 (4th ed. 1992).

B. 1. 2 Nelson & Whitman § 11.4; Nelson & Whitman casebook 946–948.

a. 1 Nelson & Whitman § 5.29; 2 Nelson & Whitman § 11.4; 4 Powell § 37.16; Raymond J. Werner, Real Estate Law §§ 20.13–20.13(m), 20.24 (11th ed. 2002); FHLMC Report, What Makes an ARM Successful? (1984); Jo Carrillo, *Dangerous Loans: Consumer Challenges to Adjustable Rate Mortgages,* 5 Berkeley Bus.L.J. 1 (2008); Janine S. Hiller & Stephen P. Ferris, *Mortgage Loan Costs: The Impact of Variable Interest Rates and Negotiability,* 18 Real Est.L.J. 259 (1990); Gary B. Tillman, Comment, *The Effect of Variable Interest Rates on Negotiability,* 48 La.L.Rev. 711 (1988); Nancy Blodgett, *Variable–Rate Notes & the UCC,* 74 A.B.A.J., Aug. 1988, at 26; 2 U.L.A. 2003 Cum. Ann. Pocket Pt. 3–5, 35–37.

b. 2 Nelson & Whitman § 11.4; Joel J. Goldberg, Note, *Alternative Mortgage Instruments: Authorizing and Implementing Price Level Adjusted Mortgages,* 16 U. Mich.J.Law Reform 115 (1982).

c. 2 Nelson & Whitman § 11.4; Ronald Friend, *Shared Appreciation Mortgages,* 34 Hastings L.J. 329 (1982); Douglas W. Kmiec, *Shared Appreciation Mortgages: A Step Toward Making Housing a Bad Investment,* 10 Real Est.L.J. 302 (1982); Michael R. Levin & Paul E. Roberts, *Future Forms of Financing: Lending Devices Addressed to Inflation and Tight Money* in Financing Real Estate in the 80s 31, 43–49 (Brian J. Strum, ed. 1981) [hereinafter Levin & Roberts].

2. 2 Nelson & Whitman § 11.4; 2 Nelson & Whitman § 11.4 (4th ed. 2002); Nelson & Whitman casebook 951–952 (6th ed. 2003).

3. Kratovil & Werner §§ 13.18–13.18(a); 1 Madison, Dwyer, & Bender § 5:17; 2 Madison, Dwyer, & Bender §§ 8:61, 11:31–11:47; J. Cary Barton & Robert E. Morrison, *Equity Participation Arrangements Between Institutional Lenders and Real Estate Developers,* 12 St. Mary's L.J. 929 (1981); Levin & Roberts 40–43; Frank E. Roegge, Gerard J. Talbot, & Robert M. Zinman, *Real Estate Equity Investments and the Institutional Lender:*

Nothing Ventured, Nothing Gained, 39 Fordham L.Rev. 579 (1971).

C. See sources cited in Ch. 6 § III.

D. 1.–3. Kratovil & Werner §§ 13.01–13.14(d); 1 Madison, Dwyer, & Bender §§ 5:21–5:23; Marion Benfield, *Money, Mortgages, and Migraine—The Usury Headache,* 19 Case W.Res.L.Rev. 819 (1968); Robert P. Lowell, *A Current Analysis of the Usury Laws: A National View,* 8 San Diego L.Rev. 193 (1971).

4. 1 Madison, Dwyer, & Bender § 5:21; Lynn M. Ewing, Jr. & Kendall R. Vickers, *Federal Pre-emption of State Usury Laws Affecting Real Estate Financing,* 47 Mo.L.Rev. 171 (1982); Samuel P. Merlo, *Federal Preemption of State Usury Statutes: Legislative and Judicial Modifications,* 99 Banking L.J. 585 (1982); Linda B. Samuels, *Usury Preemption: The Federal/State Scheme,* 98 Banking L.J. 892 (1981).

VI. Kratovil & Werner §§ 38.01–38.08; 1 Nelson & Whitman § 9.4; Robert P. Giesen, *"Routine" Mortgage Modifications: Lenders Beware,* 17 Real Est.L.J. 221 (1989).

VII. A. 1 Nelson & Whitman §§ 1.1, 6.6.

1. a. 2 Nelson & Whitman § 11.4.

b. 2 Nelson & Whitman § 11.4; 2 Nelson & Whitman § 11.4 (4th ed. 2002); Celeste M. Hammond, *Reverse Mortgages: A Financial Planning Device for the Elderly,* 1 Elder L.J. 75 (1993); Susan M. Blumenstein & Gale Harmann, Comment, *The Effect of Reverse Annuity Mortgages on SSI,* 16 U.C.Davis L.Rev. 435 (1983).

c. 2 Nelson & Whitman § 11.4; Stephen Barrett Kanner, *Growing Equity Mortgages,* 11 Real Est.L.J. 271 (1983).

2. Kratovil & Werner § 10.13; Robert Kratovil & Raymond J. Werner, Real Estate Law § 15.35(e) (8th ed. 1983); 1 Nelson & Whitman § 1.1; Raymond J. Werner, Real Estate Law §§ 20.20, 23.08 (11th ed. 2002).

3. 1 Nelson & Whitman §§ 4.17–4.19; William B. Dunn, *Selected Current Legal Issues in Mortgage Financing,* 13 Real Prop., Prob. & Tr.J. 812 (1978); Report of Comm. on Real Estate Financing, *Class Actions Under Anti–Trust Laws on Account of Escrow and Similar Practices,* 11 Real Prop., Prob. & Tr.J. 352 (1976); Henry C. Fader, Comment, *Payment of Interest on Mortgage Escrow Accounts: Judicial and Legislative Developments,* 23 Syracuse L.Rev. 845 (1972).

4.–5. Robert Kratovil, Modern Mortgage Law and Practice § 165 (1972) [hereinafter Kratovil (1972)]; Kratovil & Werner §§ 13.15(d)–13.15(e); 1 Nelson & Whitman §§ 6.8–6.10; Nelson & Whitman casebook 538–542; Steven W. Bender & Michael T. Madison, *The Enforceability of Default Interest in Real Estate Mortgages*, 43 Real Prop., Tr. & Est. L.J. 199 (2008); Paul A. Rubin, *May a*

Lender Collect Late Charges Together With Default Rate Interest?, Real Est.Fin.J., Winter 2004, at 79; Gary D. Spivey, Annotation, *Validity and Construction of Provision Imposing "Late Charge" or Similar Exaction for Delay in Making Periodic Payments on Note, Mortgage, or Installment Sale Contract*, 63 A.L.R.3d 50 (1975).

B. 1 Nelson & Whitman §§ 6.1–6.5; Penney, Broude & Cunningham 341–342; Frank S. Alexander, *Mortgage Prepayment: The Trial of Common Sense*, 72 Cornell L. Rev. 288 (1987); Debra Pogrund Stark, *Prepayment Charges in Jeopardy: The Unhappy and Uncertain Legacy of "In Re Skyler Ridge,"* 24 Real Prop., Prob. & Tr.J. 191 (1989); Alan M. Weinberger, *Neither an Early Nor a Late Payor Be?—Presuming to Question the Presumption Against Mortgage Prepayment*, 35 Wayne L.Rev. 1 (1988); John G. Wharton, *Enforceability of Prepayment Penalties in Commercial Mortgages*, 20:2 Real Est.Rev. 35 (Summer 1990); Dale A. Whitman, *Mortgage Prepayment Clauses: An Economic and Legal Analysis*, 40 UCLA L.Rev. 851 (1993); Robert K. Baldwin, Note, *Prepayment Penalties: A Survey and Suggestion*, 40 Vand. L. Rev. 409 (1987); Michael T. McNelis, Note, *Prepayment Penalties and Due-on-Sale Clauses In Commercial Mortgages: What Next?*, 20 Ind.L.Rev. 735 (1987); Ellis J. Harmon, Comment, *Secured Real Estate Loan Prepayment and the Prepayment Penalty*, 51 Cal.L.Rev. 923 (1963).

C. Kratovil & Werner §§ 34.05, 34.05(g); 1 Nelson & Whitman § 6.6; R. Wilson Freyermuth, *Why Mortgagors Can't Get No Satisfaction*, 72 Mo.L.Rev. 1159 (2007).

D. 1 Nelson & Whitman § 6.11; 4 Powell § 37.34.

CHAPTER 5. MORTGAGED PROPERTY

I. A. & B. 4 Powell § 37.13; William F. Walsh, A Treatise on Mortgages § 10 (1934) [hereinafter Walsh].

C. Kratovil & Werner § 8.01.

II. A. Kratovil & Werner § 8.06; 1 Nelson & Whitman § 9.3; 4 Powell § 37.13; Roger A. Cunningham & Saul Tischler, *Equitable Real Estate Mortgages*, 17 Rutgers L.Rev. 679, 715–723 (1963).

B. Kratovil & Werner §§ 8.03, 8.05; 4 Powell § 37.13.

C. 2 Garrard Glenn, Mortgages, Deeds of Trust, and Other Security Devices as to Land § 350 (1943) [hereinafter Glenn]; Kratovil & Werner §§ 8.02–8.02(a); 1 Nelson & Whitman §§ 9.3, 9.5; 4 Powell § 37.13.

D. Kratovil & Werner § 6.07; 1 Nelson & Whitman § 4.12.

E. 1 Nelson & Whitman §§ 4.13–4.15; Nelson & Whitman casebook 403–405, 412–413; Patrick A. Randolph, Jr., *A Mortgagee's Interest in Casualty Loss Proceeds: Evolving Rules and Risks*, 32 Real Prop., Prob., & Tr. J. 1 (1997); Derek Lisk, Comment, *Some Real Property Hazard Insurance Problems for Texas Mortgagors and Mortgagees*, 24 Hous.L.Rev. 717 (1987); Note, *Foreclosure, Loss, and the Proper Distribution of Insurance Proceeds Under Open* and Standard Mortgage Clauses: Some Observations, 7 Val.U.L.Rev. 485 (1973).

III. 1 Glenn §§ 34–34.3; 2 Glenn §§ 194–202.1; 1 Nelson & Whitman §§ 4.4, 4.10–4.11; Walsh § 22; David A. Leipziger, *The Mortgagee's Remedies For Waste,* 64 Cal.L.Rev. 1086 (1976).

CHAPTER 6. TRANSFER OF MORTGAGOR'S INTEREST

I. & II.   A., B., & C.   Kratovil & Werner §§ 1.6, 15.01–15.12; 1 Nelson & Whitman §§ 5.1–5.20; Roger A. Cunningham & Saul Tischler, *Transfer of the Real Estate Mortgagor's Interest,* 27 Rutgers L.Rev. 24 (1973); Frederic P. Storke & Don W. Sears, *Transfer of Mortgaged Property,* 38 Cornell L.Q. 185 (1953); J. Louis Warm, *Some Aspects of the Rights and Liabilities of Mortgagee, Mortgagor and Grantee,* 10 Temple L.Q. 116 (1936).

D.   1 Nelson & Whitman §§ 3.1, 3.3, 6.18–6.19.

1. 2 Arnold & Tracht §§ 6:38–6:51; Kratovil & Werner §§ 40.04–40.04(u); 2 Madison, Dwyer, & Bender §§ 12:3–12:10; 1 Nelson & Whitman §§ 3.3, 6.18–6.19; 4 Powell § 37.44; Harvey Boneparth, *Taking a Deed in Lieu of Foreclosure: Pitfalls for the Lender,* 19 Real Est.L.J. 338 (1991); Michael F. Jones, *Structuring the Deed in Lieu of Foreclosure Transaction,* 19 Real Prop., Prob. & Tr.J. 58 (1984); Richard Kelley, *Foreclosure by Contract: Deeds in Lieu of Foreclosure in Missouri,* 56 UMKC L.Rev. 633 (1988).

2. Kratovil & Werner §§ 36.01–36.05; 1 Nelson & Whitman §§ 6.15–6.17; Ann M. Burkhart, *Freeing Mortgages of Merger*, 40 Vand.L.Rev. 283 (1987).

III. & IV.   1 Nelson & Whitman §§ 5.21–5.24, 5.26, 6.5; Edward N. Barad & Leon M. Layden, *Due-on-Sale Law as Preempted by the Garn–St. Germain Act,* 12 Real Est. L.J. 138 (1983); Kent D. Coleman, *Federal Preemption of State Law Prohibitions on the Exercise of Due-on-Sale Clauses,* 100 Banking L.J. 772 (1983); William B. Dunn & Thomas S. Nowinski, *Enforcement of Due-on-Transfer Clauses: An Update,* 16 Real Prop., Prob. & Tr.J. 291 (1981); Karl E. Grier, *Due-on-Sale Clauses Under the Garn–St.Germain Depository Institutions Act of 1982,* 17 U.S.F.L.Rev. 355 (1983); Grant S. Nelson & Dale A. Whitman, *Congressional Preemption of Mortgage Due-on-Sale Law: An Analysis of the Garn–St. Germain Act,* 35 Hastings L.J. 241 (1983); Ronald R. Volkmer, *The Application of the Restraints on Alienation Doctrine to Real Property Security Interests,* 58 Iowa L.Rev. 747 (1973); Joseph Gibson, III, Note, *Due-on-Sale Clauses: Separating Social Interests from Individual Interests,* 35 Vand.L.Rev. 357 (1982); Report of

Subcomm. on "Due-on" Clauses of Comm. on Real Estate Financing, *Enforcement of Due-on-Transfer Clauses,* 13 Real Prop., Prob. & Tr.J. 891 (1978); FHLBB Regulations, *Preemption of State Due-on-Sale Laws,* 48 Fed.Regis. 21554–21563 (1983).

V. 2 Glenn §§ 300–307; Osborne § 251; 4 Powell § 37.30[6]; J. Kraut, Annotation, *Right of Heir or Devisee to Have Realty Exonerated From Lien Thereon at Expense of Personal Estate,* 4 A.L.R.3d 1023 (1965).

CHAPTER 7. TRANSFER OF MORTGAGEE'S INTEREST

I. & II.   A.—C.   1 Nelson & Whitman §§ 5.27–5.28; 4 Powell § 37.27.

D.   1 Nelson & Whitman §§ 5.28; 4 James J. White & Robert S. Summers, Uniform Commercial Code §§ 30–7, 30–8, 31–5, 31–7, 33–10 (5th ed. 2002 & Supp. 2007) [hereinafter White & Summers]; W. Rodney Clement, Jr. & Baxter Dunaway, *Revised Article 9 and Real Property,* 36 Real Prop., Prob. & Tr. J. 511 (2001) [hereinafter Clement & Dunaway, *Revised Article 9*]; Phillip H Ebling & Steven O. Weise, *What a Dirt Lawyer Needs to Know About New Article 9 of the UCC,* 37 Real Prop., Prob. & Tr. J. 191 (2002) [hereinafter Ebling & Weise, *What a Dirt Lawyer Needs to Know*]; Gary A. Goodman, *Revised UCC Article 9: Its Broad and Varied Impact on Real Estate Finance,* Real Est. Fin. J., Fall 2000 at 11; Julian B. McDonnell & John Franklin Hitchcock, Jr., *The Sale of Promissory Notes Under Revised Article 9: Cooking Securitization Stew,* 117 Banking L.J. 99 (2000) [hereinafter McDonnell & Hitchcock, *The Sale of Promissory Notes Under Revised Article 9*]; UCC §§ 9–309 cmt. 4, 9–330 cmt. 7.

E.   Baxter Dunaway, The Law of Distressed Real Estate §§ 24:19–24:20 (Sept. 2008) [hereinafter Dunaway]; Kratovil & Werner § 32.02; 1 Nelson & Whitman § 5.34; R.K. Arnold, *Yes, There is Life on MERS,* Prob. & Prop., July/Aug. 1997, at 32; Ebling & Weise, *What a Dirt Lawyer Needs to Know*; Phyllis K. Slesinger & Daniel Mclaughlin, *Mortgage Electronic Registration System,* 31 Idaho L.Rev. 805 (1995).

F.   1 Nelson & Whitman § 5.27; 4 Powell § 37.27.

III.   Dunaway § 24:96; Kratovil & Werner §§ 32.05, 32.06; Fred H. Miller & Alvin C. Harrell, The Law of Modern Payments Systems and Notes §§ 3.03, 6.01–6.03 (Practitioner's Edition 2002 & Supp. 2007) [hereinafter Miller & Harrell]; Nelson & Whitman §§ 5.27–5.32; Osborne §§ 227–228, 231; Richard E. Speidel & Steve H. Nickles, Negotiable Instruments and Check Collection (the new law) in a Nutshell 289–363 (4th ed. 1993); UCC §§ 3–302 cmts. 1–3, 3–305 cmts. 1–2.

IV.   Dunaway § 19.23 (1996), §§ 24:93–24:95 (Sept. 2008); Kratovil & Werner §§ 34.01–34.01(e); Miller & Harrell § 6.03[6][b]; 1 Nelson & Whitman §§ 5.33–5.34; Nelson & Whitman casebook 501–507; Grant S. Nelson & Dale A. Whitman, Real Estate

Finance Law §§ 5.33–5.34 (Hornbook Series—2d ed. 1985); Osborne §§ 233–237; Clement & Dunaway, *Revised Article 9*; Dale A. Whitman, *Reforming the Law; The Payment Rule as a Paradigm*, 1998 B.Y.U. L.Rev. 1169; Annotation, *Recording Laws as Applied to Assignments of Mortgages on Real Estate*, 89 A.L.R. 171 (1934); UCC § 3–602 cmts. 2–3.

V. Kratovil & Werner § 32.10; 1 Nelson & Whitman § 5.34; Nelson & Whitman casebook 504; 4 White & Summers § 33–10; Clement & Dunaway, *Revised Article 9*; Ebling & Weise, *What a Dirt Lawyer Needs to Know*; McDonnell & Hitchcock, *The Sale of Promissory Notes Under Revised Article 9*; UCC § 9–330 cmt. 7.

VI. A. & B. Kratovil & Werner § 33.01; 2 Madison, Dwyer, & Bender §§ 11:1–11:6, 11:8–11:29; 1 Nelson & Whitman § 5.35; Nelson & Whitman casebook 507–512; Osborne § 243; 4 Powell § 37.29.

C. 2 Glenn § 317; 1 Nelson & Whitman § 5.35; 4 Powell § 37.29.

D. 2 Glenn §§ 318–318.3; 1 Nelson & Whitman § 5.35; Osborne §§ 244–246.

VII. Kratovil & Werner §§ 31.01–31.07; 2 Nelson & Whitman §§ 10.1–10.8; Osborne §§ 282, 284; Restatement (Third) of Property—Mortgages § 7.6(b)(4) & cmt. e (1997); Grant S. Nelson & Dale A. Whitman, *Adopting Restatement Mortgage Subrogation Principles: Saving Billions of Dollars for Refinancing Homeowners*, 2006 B.Y.U.L.Rev. 305; John C. Murray, *Equitable Subrogation: Is the Trend Toward the Restatement Approach*, Prob. & Prop., Nov./Dec. 2007 at 19.

VIII. 1 Nelson & Whitman §§ 5.27–5.28; Nelson & Whitman casebook 499–501, 505–507; 4 White & Summers §§ 30–7, 30–8, 31–5, 31–7, 33–10; Clement & Dunaway, *Revised Article 9*; Ebling & Weise, *What a Dirt Lawyer Needs to Know*; UCC §§ 9–109 cmt. 7; 9–308 cmt. 6.

IX. 2 Glenn § 311; 4 Powell § 37.23.

CHAPTER 8. AFTER DEFAULT AND BEFORE FORECLOSURE

I. A. & B. Kratovil & Werner § 14.05; 1 Nelson & Whitman § 7.6; Osborne § 325.

C. Kratovil & Werner § 14.04; 1 Nelson & Whitman § 7.7; E. J. Spires, Annotation, *Acceptance of Past–Due Interest as Waiver of Acceleration Clause in Note or Mortgage*, 97 A.L.R.2d 997 (1964).

II. Kratovil & Werner §§ 14.01–14.07, 14.09–14.10; 1 Nelson & Whitman §§ 7.6–7.8; Bruce J. Bergman, *Strict Acceleration in New York Mortgage Foreclosure—Has the Doctrine Eroded?*, 8 Pace L.Rev. 475 (1988); Robert R. Rosenthal, *The Role of Courts of Equity in Preventing Acceleration Predicated Upon a Mortgagor's Inadvertent Default*, 22 Syracuse L.Rev. 897 (1971).

III. A. Kratovil & Werner, §§ 20.01–20.02; 1 Nelson & Whitman §§ 1.5, 4.1–4.3, 4.20; Osborne, §§ 13–16; Report of Comm. on Mortgage Law & Practice, *Disposition of Rents and Profits After Mortgage Default*, 2 Real Prop., Prob. & Tr.J. 601 (1967).

B. 1.–3. 1 Glenn § 33.3; 2 Glenn §§ 203–204.1; Kratovil & Werner §§ 20.02–20.03(g); 1 Nelson & Whitman §§ 4.24–4.32.

4. 1 Glenn § 33.4; Kratovil & Werner §§ 20.04–20.05(c); 1 Nelson & Whitman §§ 4.20–4.23; 2 Nelson & Whitman § 12.9; Robert Kratovil, *Mortgages—Problems in Possession, Rents and Mortgagee Liability*, 11 DePaul L.Rev. 1 (1961); Robert D. Feinstein & Sidney A. Keyles, *Foreclosure: Subordination, Non–Disturbance and Attornment Agreements*, Prob. & Prop., July–Aug. 1989, at 38.

C. Kratovil & Werner §§ 20.07–20.07(a); 2 Madison, Dwyer, & Bender §§ 12:13–12:16; 1 Nelson & Whitman §§ 4.35, 4.39, 8.18; Nelson & Whitman casebook 363–367; Julia Patterson Forrester, *Still Crazy After All These Years: The Absolute Assignment of Rents in Mortgage Loan Transactions*, 59 Fla.L.Rev. 487 (2007); Julia Patterson Forrester, *A Uniform and More Rational Approach to Rents as Security for the Mortgage Loan*, 46 Rutgers L.Rev. 349 (1993); R. Wilson Freyermuth, *Modernizing Security in Rents: The New Uniform Assignment of Rents Act*, 71 Mo.L.Rev. 1 (2006); Uniform Assignment of Rents Act, Prefatory Note (2005); http://www.nccusl.org/Update/uniformact_factsheets/uniformacts-fs-vara.asp (last visited Sept. 17, 2008).

D. Dunaway §§ 11:35–11:36; Kratovil & Werner §§ 20.03, 20.06; 1 Nelson & Whitman §§ 4.33–4.43; 4 Powell § 37.39; Robert K. Lifton, *Real Estate in Trouble: Lender's Remedies Need an Overhaul*, 31 Bus. Law. 1927 (1976); Comment, The Mortgagee's Right to Rents After Default, 50 Yale L.J. 1424 (1941); J.P. Ludington, Annotation, *Propriety of Appointing Receiver, At Behest of Mortgagee, To Manage or Operate Property During Foreclosure Action*, 82 A.L.R.2d 1075 (1962).

IV. 1 Nelson & Whitman §§ 6.6, 7.1–7.5; Marshall E. Tracht, *Renegotiation and Secured Credit: Explaining the Equity of Redemption*, 52 Vand. L.Rev. 599 (1999).

V. A. & B. 2 Arnold & Tracht §§ 6:38–6:92; Kratovil & Werner §§ 40.01(a)–40.07; 2 Madison, Dwyer, & Bender §§ 12:1–12:10; Real Estate Bankruptcies and Workouts (A. Kuklin & P. Roberts eds. 1983); John C. Murray, *Mortgage Workouts: Deeds in Escrow*, 41 Real Prop., Prob. & Tr.J. 185 (2006); Paul E. Roberts & Howard J. Lazarus, *When the Workout Doesn't Work Out—An Outline*, 12 Real Prop., Prob. & Tr.J. 437 (1977).

C. 2 Madison, Dwyer, & Bender, §§ 12:2, 12:10; David Schmudde, *Lessons from the Subprime Mortgage Debacle*, Prac. Real Est.Law., May 2008, at 9; Ruth Simon & James R. Hagerty, *Why Lenders Are Leery of Short Sales*, Wall St.J., April 17, 2008, at D1; David Streitfeld, *Coming Up Short*, N.Y. Times, Sept. 19, 2008, at C1; James R.

Hagerty & Ruth Simon, *Home Loans 'Under Water' Grow, Pressure the Economy*, Wall St.J., Oct. 8, 2008, at 1.

D. 1 Glenn §§ 73–73.1, 96; 1 Nelson & Whitman §§ 8.1–8.2.

CHAPTER 9. PRIORITIES

I. Walsh §§ 74, 79.

II. William E. Burby, Handbook of the Law of Real Property §§ 130–134 (3d ed. 1965); Barlow Burke, Law of Title Insurance § 2.01 (3d ed. 2008); John E. Cribbet & Corwin W. Johnson, Principles of the Law of Property 306–326 (3d ed. 1989); 1 Nelson & Whitman § 5.35; 1 Joyce Palomar, Title Insurance Law § 1:3 (2007).

III.   A. Kratovil & Werner §§ 19.01–19.09; 1 Nelson & Whitman, §§ 1.1, 9.1.

B. Kratovil & Werner, §§ 30.01–30.08; 2 Nelson & Whitman §§ 12.9–12.10; Osborne § 212; Restatement (Third) of Property—Mortgages § 7.7 cmt. c. (1997); Gerald Korngold, *Construction Loan Advances and the Subordinated Purchase Money Mortgagee: An Appraisal, A Suggested Approach, and the ULTA Perspective,* 50 Fordham L.Rev. 313 (1981); Hugh B. Lambe, *Enforceability of Subordination Agreements,* 19 Real Prop., Prob. & Tr.J. 631 (1984); Warren H. McNamara, Jr., *Subordination Agreements as Viewed by Sellers, Purchasers, Construction Lenders, and Title Companies,* 12 Real Est.L.J. 347 (1984); Frederick D. Minnes, Note, *Purchase Money Subordination Agreements in California: An Analysis of Conventional Subordination,* 45 S.Cal.L.Rev. 1109 (1972); George Hollodick, Note, *Real Estate Finance—Subordination Clauses: North Carolina Subordinates Substance to Form—"MCB Ltd. v. McGowan,"* 23 Wake Forest L.Rev. 575 (1988); David J. Marchitelli, Annotation, *Construction Mortgagee–Lender's Duty to Protect Interest of Subordinated Purchase–Money Mortgagee,* 13 ALR5th 684 (1993); B. P. O'Byrne, Annotation, *Specific Performance: Requisite Definiteness of Provision in Contract for Sale or Lease of Land, That Vendor or Landlord Will Subordinate His Interest to Permit Other Party to Obtain Financing,* 26 A.L.R.3d 855 (1969).

C. Richard B. Hagedorn, Secured Transactions in a Nutshell 263–270 (5th ed. 2007); Ray D. Henson, Handbook on Secured Transactions Under the Uniform Commercial Code, §§ 4–19, 8–1 to 8–3 (2d ed. 1979); Kratovil & Werner §§ 9.01–9.11; 1 Nelson & Whitman §§ 9.5–9.7; Daniel Fenton Adams, *Security Interests in Fixtures Under Mississippi's Uniform Commercial Code,* 47 Miss.L.J. 831 (1976); David Gray Carlson, *Fixture Priorities,* 4 Cardozo L.Rev. 381 (1983); U.C.C. §§ 9–313 cmts. 1–8, 9–403 cmt. 4 (1990); U.C.C. §§ 9–334 cmts. 1–7, 11, 9–501 cmt. 2, 9–519 cmt. 2 (2007).

D. 1.–3. Kratovil § 214 (1972); Kratovil & Werner §§ 25.27–25.27(c); 1 Madison, Dwyer, & Bender §§ 6:14–6:15; 2 Nelson & Whitman § 12.4; 5 Powell §§ P3A.08, 38.10–38.18; Ethan Glass, *Old Statutes Never Die . . . Nor Do They Fade Away: A Proposal for Modernizing Mechanics' Lien Law by Federal Action,* 27 Ohio N.U. L.Rev. 67

(2000) [hereinafter Glass, *Old Statutes*]; Kratovil & Werner, *Mortgages for Construction and the Lien Priorities Problem—The "Unobligatory" Advance*, 41 Tenn. L. Rev. 311 (1974); Blake Nelson, *Construction Liens: A National Review and Template for a Uniform Lien Act*, 34 Wm.Mitchell L.Rev. 245 (2007); Michael G. Walsh, *A Mechanics' Lien Primer for the General Practitioner*, Prac. Law., July 1991, at 77; Uniform Simplification of Land Transfers Act, Introductory Comment to Article 5 (1977).

4. 2 Nelson & Whitman § 12.5; Glass, *Old Statutes*; Stephen C. Skubel, Note, *Mechanics' Liens Subject to Fourteenth Amendment Guarantees*, 26 Cath.U.L.Rev. 129 (1976); Denzil F. Lowry, Jr., Commentary, *Creditors' Rights: The Constitutionality of Oklahoma's Mechanics' Lien Law*, 31 Okla.L.Rev. 148 (1978).

5. Kratovil & Werner § 25.28: 1 Madison, Dwyer, & Bender § 6:17; 2 Nelson & Whitman § 12.6; 5 Powell § 38.19; Russell M. Blain, Note, *Lien Rights and Construction Lending: Responsibilities and Liabilities in Florida*, 29 U.Fla.L.Rev. 411 (1977); Richard Paroutaud, Note, *Mechanics' Liens: The "Stop Notice" Comes to Washington*, 49 Wash.L.Rev. 685 (1974).

E. 1. 3 Glenn §§ 434–435; 1 Nelson & Whitman § 4.17; 5 Powell §§ P3A.03; 39.02–39.04.

2. Kratovil §§ 422–429 (1972); 5 Powell § 39.05; 25 Fed. Tax Coordinator 2d ¶¶ V–6300 to V–6454 (2008).

F. 1 Nelson & Whitman § 7.13.

G. 2 Glenn §§ 289–296; Kratovil & Werner §§ 16.04, 34.05(h), 41.09(n); 2 Madison, Dwyer, & Bender § 8:19; 2 Nelson & Whitman §§ 10.09–10.15; Walsh §§ 55–56; Frederic P. Storke & Don W. Sears, *Transfer of Mortgaged Property*, 38 Cornell L.Q 185 (1953); John J. Shalhoub, Note, *Marshaling: Equitable Rights of Holders of Junior Interests*, 38 Rutgers L.Rev. 287 (1986).

CHAPTER 10. FORECLOSURE

I. Kratovil & Werner §§ 41.04, 41.09(c); 1 Nelson & Whitman § 7.12; 4 Powell §§ 37.36, 37.37[6]; Walsh § 74.

II. 1 Nelson & Whitman §§ 6.11, 6.14.

III.   A. 2 Madison, Dwyer, & Bender §§ 13:1–13:41; 1 Nelson & Whitman §§ 8.12–8.19; Thomas R. Califano & Timothy W. Walsh, *Real Estate Lenders and Landlords are Winners in Bankruptcy Code Amendments*, Real Est.Fin.J., Fall 2005, at 23; Baxter Dunaway, *Effect of the Bankruptcy Reform Act of 1994 on Real Estate*, 30 Real Prop., Prob. & Tr.J. 601 (1996); Frank R. Kennedy, *Involuntary Fraudulent Transfers*, 9 Cardozo L.Rev. 531 (1987); Patrick E. Mears & John T. Gregg, *What Congress Hath Wrought: Provisions of the Bankruptcy Abuse Prevention and Consumer Protection Act Affecting Interests in Real Estate*, Prob. & Prop., Nov./Dec. 2005, at 23; John C.

Murray, *The New Bankruptcy Act: Observations on Some of the Provisions Affecting Real Estate,* Prob. & Prop., Nov./Dec. 2005, at 43; Debra Pogrund Stark, *The Emperor Still Has Clothes: Fraudulent Conveyance Challenges After the BFP Decision,* 47 S.C.L.Rev. 563 (1996); Catherine M. Stites, Note, *A Palace for a Peppercorn: A Post–BFP Proposal to Resurrect Section 548(A)(2)(A),* 73 Wash. U.L.Q. 1747 (1995).

B.   Kratovil & Werner §§ 41.05–41.05(c); 1 Nelson & Whitman §§ 8.9–8.11; Philip J. Bagley, III, *The Soldiers' and Sailors' Civil Relief Act—A Survey,* 45 Mil.L.Rev. 1 (1969); Kathleen H. Switzer, *Mortgage Defaults and the Soldiers' and Sailors' Civil Relief Act: Assigning the Burden of Proof When Applying the Material Effect Test,* 18 Real Est.L.J. 171 (1989); *Military and Civil Defense,* 53A Am.Jur.2d §§ 352–355 (2006); W. E. Shipley, Annotation, *Soldiers' and Sailors' Civil Relief Act of 1940, As Amended, As Affecting Foreclosure of Mortgages and Trust Deeds,* 40 A.L.R.2d 1262 (1955).

IV.   Kratovil & Werner § 41.09; 1 Nelson & Whitman §§ 1.4, 7.11, 7.12; Osborne § 318; Foreclosure Law & Related Remedies: A State–By–State Digest (Sidney A. Keyles, ed., 1995).

A.   1.   Kratovil & Werner § 41.09(c); 1 Nelson & Whitman §§ 7.12, 7.14; Osborne § 321; 4 Powell § 37.37[6]; Walsh §§ 68, 74.

2.   Kratovil & Werner § 20.05; 1 Nelson & Whitman § 7.12; Robert D. Feinstein & Sidney A. Keyles, *Foreclosure: Subordination, Non–Disturbance and Attornment Agreements,* Prob. & Prop., July–Aug. 1989, at 38.

3.   1 Nelson & Whitman § 7.13.

B. & C.   Kratovil & Werner §§ 41.09(h)–41.09(o); 1 Nelson & Whitman § 7.16; 4 Powell § 37.40; Robert M. Washburn, *The Judicial and Legislative Response to Price Inadequacy in Mortgage Foreclosure Sales,* 53 S.Cal.L.Rev. 843 (1980).

D.   1.   1 Glenn § 94; 1 Nelson & Whitman §§ 1.1, 7.17; Walsh § 74.

2.   1 Nelson & Whitman § 7.15; George M. Platt, *The Dracula Mortgage: Creature of the Omitted Junior Lienholder,* 67 Or.L.Rev. 287 (1988).

3.   1 Glenn § 94.1; Kratovil & Werner § 41.09(m).

4.   Kratovil & Werner § 41.16; 1 Nelson & Whitman § 4.44; Grant S. Nelson, *The Foreclosure Purchase by the Equity of Redemption Holder or Other Junior Interests: When Should Principles of Fairness and Morality Trump Normal Priority Rules?,* 72 Mo.L.Rev. 1259 (2007).

E.   Kratovil & Werner § 41.09(p); 1 Nelson & Whitman §§ 1.1, 7.31–7.32; 4 Powell § 37.41; Walsh § 79.

F.   Kratovil & Werner § 41.10, 1 Nelson & Whitman §§ 8.1, 8.3; 4 Powell §§ 37.36, 37.41; Walsh § 77; John Mixon,

> *Deficiency Judgments Following Home Mortgage Foreclo-
> sure: An Anachronism That Increases Personal Tragedy,
> Impedes Regional Economic Recovery, and Means Little to
> Lenders,* 22 Texas Tech.L.Rev. 1 (1991); Robert M. Wash-
> burn, *The Judicial and Legislative Response to Price
> Inadequacy in Mortgage Foreclosure Sales,* 53 S.Cal.
> L.Rev. 843 (1980).

V. Kratovil & Werner §§ 41.08–41.08(a)(1), 41.09; 1 Nelson & Whitman §§ 1.4, 7.9, 7.19; 4 Powell § 37.42[1]–[6]; Foreclosure Law &
Related Remedies: A State–By–State Digest (Sidney A. Keyles, ed.,
1995).

    A. Kratovil & Werner §§ 41.08–41.08(c), 41.08(e)–41.08(p); 1
Nelson & Whitman §§ 7.19–7.22, 8.1; Nelson & Whitman
casebook 630–631; Osborne §§ 342–344; 4 Powell
§ 37.42[1]–[6].

    B. 1 Nelson & Whitman §§ 7.23–7.30; James M. Pedowitz,
Current Developments in Summary Foreclosure, 9 Real
Prop., Prob. & Tr.J. 421 (1974); Daniel E. Blegen, Note,
*The Constitutionality of Power of Sale Foreclosures by
Federal Government Entities,* 62 Mo.L.Rev. 425 (1997);
Donald L. Schwartz, Comment, *Power of Sale Foreclosure
After Fuentes,* 40 U.Chi.L.Rev. 206 (1972).

VI. 1 Nelson & Whitman §§ 1.3, 7.9–7.10; Osborne §§ 311, 314–315; 4
Powell § 37.43; James Geoffrey Durham, *In Defense of Strict Foreclosure: A Legal and Economic Analysis of Mortgage Foreclosure,*
36 S.C.Law Rev. 461 (1985).

VII. 2 Glenn §§ 227–243; Kratovil & Werner §§ 42.06–42.17; 1 Nelson
& Whitman §§ 1.4, 7.1, 8.4–8.7; Nelson & Whitman casebook 603;
Osborne §§ 8, 307–310; 4 Powell § 37.46; Patrick B. Bauer, *Judi-
cial Foreclosure and Statutory Redemption: The Soundness of
Iowa's Traditional Preference for Protection Over Credit,* 71 Iowa
L.Rev. 1 (1985); Patrick B. Bauer, *Statutory Redemption Reconsid-
ered: The Operation of Iowa's Redemption Statute in Two Counties
Between 1881 and 1980,* 70 Iowa L.Rev. 343 (1985); Catherine A.
Gnatek, Note, *The New Mortgage Foreclosure Law: Redemption
and Reinstatement,* 1989 U.Ill.L.Rev. 471; Benjamin Pitts, Com-
ment, *Waiver of Redemption Rights in Tennessee Mortgages: Dis-
carding the Contracts Clause and Common–Law Concepts,* 55 Tenn.
L.Rev. 733 (1988); James Timothy Payne, Annotation, *Mortgages:
Effect on Subordinate Lien of Redemption by Owner or Assignee
From Sale Under Prior Lien,* 56 A.L.R.4th 703 (1987).

VIII. James H. Carr & Kate Davidoff, *Legislative and Regulatory Re-
sponses to the Foreclosure Crisis,* 17 J. Affordable Housing &
Community Dev. L. 283 (2008); Creola Johnson, *Stealing the Amer-
ican Dream: Can Foreclosure-Rescue Companies Circumvent New
Laws Designed to Protect Homeowners from Equity Theft?,* 2007
Wis.L.Rev. 649; Howard F. Mulligan & Jennifer B. Lawrence, *The
Mortgage Reform and Anti–Predatory Lending Act of 2007: The
Push for Assignee Liability and Navigating the Protections of a Safe
Harbor,* Real Est.Fin.J., Spring 2008, at 44; Christopher Rosen-
bleeth, *Legislative and Other Responses to Subprime Crisis,* Real
Est.Fin.J., Spring 2008, at 61; David Schmudde, *Lessons from the*

Subprime Mortgage Debacle, Prac. Real Est.Law., May 2008, at 9;
Vikas Bajaj, *Housing Lenders Fear Bigger Wave of Loan Defaults*,
N.Y. Times, Aug. 4, 2008, at A1; Tripp Baltz, *Colorado Legislature
Sends Governor Foreclosure Transparency Legislation*, Banking Da-
ily, May 15, 2008; Nicholas Confessore & Jeremy W. Peters, *A
Proposal from Albany on Stemming Foreclosures*, N.Y. Times, June
20, 2008, at A21; Michael Corkery, *Slowing Foreclosures May Mask
Breadth of Woes*, Wall St.J., Aug. 11, 2008, at A2; James R.
Hagerty, Ruth Simon & Damian Paletta, *U.S. Seizes Mortgage
Giants*, Wall St.J., Sept. 8, 2008, at 1; James R. Hagerty, Deborah
Solomon, & Sudeep Reddy, *Treasury, Fed Affirm Backing for Ailing
Mortgage Giants*, Wall St.J., July 14, 2008, at A1; David M. Hersz-
enhorn, *Senate Passes Housing Legislation That Raises the Na-
tion's Debt Limit,* N.Y. Times, July 27, 2008, at 16; *The Housing
Bill*, N.Y. Times, July 27, 2008 at 16; Stephen Labaton, *Loan
Industry Fighting Rules on Mortgages*, N.Y.Times, April 28, 2008,
at A1; Stephen Labaton, *Treasury Unveils Vast Plan to Save
Mortgage Giants*, N.Y.Times, July 14, 2008, at A1; Stephen Laba-
ton & Edmund L. Andrews, *In Rescue, U.S. Takes Over Mortgage
Finance Titans: A Costly Bailout,* N.Y. Times, Sept. 8, 2008, at A1;
John Leland, *Foreclosures Push States to Try a Mix of Solutions*,
N.Y. Times, April 16, 2008, at A14; Laura Mahoney, *California
Senate OKs Weakened Version of Bill Targeting at Subprime Fore-
closures*, Banking Daily, April 30, 2008; Ruth Simon & Amy Mer-
rick, *States Move Fast on Mortgage Aid*, Wall St.J., April 4, 2008, at
A2; Mark Wolski, *Minnesota Governor Vetoes Mortgage Bill: Would
Defer Foreclosures Up to One Year,* Banking Daily, June 2, 2008;
*States Stepping Up Oversight of Lenders to Address Subprime
Crisis*, 35 No. CD–17 HDR Current Developments 2 (Sept. 3, 2007).

**CHAPTER 11. FINANCING COOPERATIVES AND CONDOMINI-
UMS**

I.–III.   1 Arnold & Tracht §§ 4:101–4:113, 4:126–4:128.50, 4:129—4:138;
Kratovil & Werner §§ 26.01–26.14; 2 Madison, Dwyer, & Bender
§§ 10:1–10:15; 2 Nelson & Whitman §§ 13.1–13.6; 4B Powell
¶ ¶ 631–632.1[6], 632.3, 632.4[2]–[3], 632.5[3]–[5] (1996); Patrick
J. Rohan & Melvin A. Reskin, 1,Pt.1 & 1,Pt.2 Condominium Law
and Practice §§ 1.01–1.05, 3.01–3.04, 7.01–7.12, 9.01–9.09, 12.01–
12.07 (2008—Release No. 96, June 2008); Patrick J. Rohan &
Melvin A. Reskin, 2 Cooperative Housing Law and Practice
§§ 1.01–2.03, 5.01, 5A.01–5A.04 (2003—Release No. 56, Aug.
2003); Marvin Garfinkel, *The Uniform Condominium Act,* Prac.
Law., Dec. 1982, at 43; Richard J. Kane, *The Financing of Cooperatives and Condominiums: A Retrospective*, 73 St. John's L. Rev.
101 (1999); T. Bertram King, *Problems of Financing Condominiums,* 24 Bus.Law. 445 (1969); Thomas Pfeiler, *Condominium
Financing: Some Legal Basics,* 38 U.S.Sav. & Loan League Legal
Bull. 249 (1972); William Griffith Thomas, *The New Uniform
Condominium Act,* 64 A.B.A.J. 1370 (1978); Uniform Condominium Act, Prefatory Note & § 3–116 cmt. 2 (1980); *Table of Juris-*

dictions Wherein [Uniform Condominium] Act Has Been Adopted, *7, Pt. II U.L.A. 200 (Supp.2007).*

CHAPTER 12. REFORM

I. & II. A. D. Barlow Burke, Jr., Law of Federal Mortgage Documents §§ 1.1.4–1.1.8, 1.3–1.5, 11.1–11.4 (1989 & Supp. 1995); Kratovil & Werner §§ 6.02–6.03; 6.23–6.24(a); 37.02–37.03; 1 Nelson & Whitman §§ 7.19, 8.8; 2 Nelson & Whitman §§ 11.3, 11.5-11.6; Frank S. Alexander, *Federal Intervention in Real Estate Finance: Preemption and Federal Common Law,* 71 N.C.L.Rev. 293 (1993); Ann M. Burkhart, *Real Estate Practice in the Twenty–First Century,* 72 Mo.L.Rev. 1031 (2007); Julia Patterson Forrester, *Fannie Mae/Freddie Mac Uniform Mortgage Instruments: The Forgotten Benefit to Homeowners,* 72 Mo.L.Rev. 1077 (2007); Eric T. Freyfogle, *The New Judicial Roles in Illinois Mortgage Foreclosures,* 19 Loy.U.Chi.L.J. 933 (1988); Alex M. Johnson, Jr., *Critiquing the Foreclosure Process: An Economic Approach Based on the Paradigmatic Norms of Bankruptcy,* 79 Va. L.Rev. 959 (1993); David M. Madway & Daniel D. Pearlman, *Mortgage Forms and Foreclosure Practices: Time for Reform,* 9 Real Prop., Prob. & Tr.J. 560 (1974); Basil H. Mattingly, *The Shift from Power to Process: A Functional Approach to Foreclosure Law,* 80 Marq. L.Rev. 77 (1996); Grant S. Nelson, *A Commerce Clause Standard for the New Millennium: "Yes" to Congressional Control over Commercial Transactions; "No" to Federal Legislation on Social and Cultural Issues,* 55 Ark.L.Rev.1213 (2003) [hereinafter Nelson, *A Commerce Clause Standard for the New Millennium*]; James M. Pedowitz, *Current Developments in Summary Foreclosure,* 9 Real Prop., Prob. & Tr.J. 421 (1974); Paul J. Prinzivalli, *Federal Legislation Preempts State Laws; Statutes Only Affect HUD Mortgages, N.Y.L.J.,* Aug. 21, 1995, at S3; Patrick A. Randolph, Jr., *The New Federal Foreclosure Laws,* 49 Okla.L.Rev. 123 (1996); Debra Pogrund Stark, *Facing the Facts: An Empirical Study of the Fairness and Efficiency of Foreclosures and a Proposal for Reform,* 30 U.Mich.J.L.Reform 639 (1997); Debra Pogrund Stark, *Foreclosing on the American Dream: An Evaluation of State and Federal Foreclosure Laws,* 51 Okla.L.Rev. 229 (1998); Steven Wechsler, *Through the Looking Glass: Foreclosure by Sale as "De Facto" Strict Foreclosure—An Empirical Study of Mortgage Foreclosure and Subsequent Resale,* 70 Cornell L.Rev. 850 (1985); Report of Comm. on Mortgage Law & Practice, *Cost and Time Factors in Foreclosure of Mortgages,* 3 Real Prop., Prob. & Tr.J. 413 (1968); Uniform Land Transaction Act, Introductory Comment to Article 3 (1977); Uniform Land Security Interest Act, Prefatory Note (1985); S. Rep. No. 103–307, at 86–89 (1994); *Testimony Concerning Debt Collection Improvement Act of 1995 Before House Comm. on Gov't Mgmt., Info. & Tech.* (statement of Gerald

Stern, Special Couns. for Fin. Institution Fraud, Off. of Deputy Att'y Gen.), 1995 WL 561205 (F.D.C.H.).

B. 4 Powell ¶ 435.1, § 37.42[1]–[6]; Roger Bernhardt, *ULSIA's Remedies on Default—Worth the Effort?*, 24 Conn.L.Rev. 1001 (1992); Jon W. Bruce, *Mortgage Law Reform Under the Uniform Land Transactions Act,* 64 Geo.L.J. 1245 (1976); Norman Geis, *Escape From the 15th Century: The Uniform Land Security Interest Act,* 30 Real Prop., Prob. & Tr.J. 289 (1995); James M. Pedowitz, *Mortgage Foreclosure Under ULSIA (Uniform Land Security Interest Act),* 27 Wake Forest L.Rev. 495 (1992); James M. Pedowitz, *Mortgage Foreclosure Under the Uniform Land Transactions Act (As Amended),* 6 Real Est.L.J. 179 (1978); Patrick A. Randolph, Jr., *The Future of American Real Estate Law: Uniform Foreclosure Laws and Uniform Land Security Interest Act,* 20 Nova L.Rev. 1109 (1996); Uniform Land Transactions Act, Prefatory Note, Introductory Comment to Article 3, & Comments to §§ 3–101 to 3–513 (1977); Uniform Land Security Interest Act, Prefatory Note & Comments to §§ 101–514 (1985).

C. Nelson, *A Commerce Clause Standard for the New Millennium*; Grant S. Nelson & Dale A. Whitman, *Reforming Foreclosure: The Uniform Nonjudicial Foreclosure Act,* 53 Duke L.J. 1399 (2004); Dale A. Whitman, *Chinese Mortgage Law: An American Perspective,* 15 Colum. J. Asian L. 35 (2001); Uniform Nonjudicial Foreclosure Act, Prefatory Note (2002); http://www.nccusl.org/Update/uniformact_factsheets/uniformacts-fs-unfa.asp (last visited Sept. 17, 2008).

D. Restatement (Third) of Property—Mortgages, Introduction (1997); Dale A. Whitman, *Mortgage Drafting: Lessons from the Restatement of Mortgages*, 33 Real Prop., Prob. & Tr. J. 415 (1998).

INDEX

References are to Pages

269

†